THE PILLARS OF ISLAM

Frances Gumley was the first woman editor of the *Catholic Herald* before becoming a producer of religious programmes for the BBC. She is now a freelance producer for Radio Four and Channel Four. She is the co-author, with Brian Redhead, of *The Good Book* and *The Christian Centuries*.

Brian Redhead is a well-known broadcaster who regularly presents the *Today* programme on Radio Four. His books include *Plato to Nato*, *A Love of the Lakes*, *Northumbria* and *The Peak – a Park for all Seasons*.

THE
PILLARS
◇ OF ◇
ISLAM

An introduction to the Islamic faith

FRANCES GUMLEY
&
BRIAN REDHEAD

BBC Books

The quotations from the Qur'an
in this book have been taken from
*The Glorious Koran: A bi-lingual edition with
English translation, introduction and notes* by
Marmaduke Pickthall, published by Allen & Unwin,
London 1976 (first edition published in 1930).

Published by BBC Books,
a division of BBC Enterprises Limited,
Woodlands, 80 Wood Lane, London W12 0TT
First Published 1990

Reprinted 1990

ISBN 0 563 20879 1

Set in 11/13½ Bembo by Ace Filmsetting Ltd, Frome
Printed in England by Clays Ltd, St Ives plc
Cover printed by Clays Ltd, St Ives plc

CONTENTS

1

The Prophet

Lo! We revealed it on the Night of Power.
Ah, what will convey unto thee what the Night of
  Power is!
The Night of Power is better than a thousand months.
The angels and the Spirit descend therein, by the
  permission of their Lord, with all decrees.
(That night is) Peace until the rising of the dawn.

Sura 97, Power

Five times every day one-fifth of the world's population is
called to prayer. Whether in Baghdad or in Birmingham, in
Bokhara or Brisbane, those obeying the call kneel down and
turn their faces to the holy city of Mecca, the navel of the
world, where, they believe, Adam, the first man and the first
prophet of Islam, built the world's earliest sanctuary to the
unseen God. But that summons to prayer is not as old as
Adam. It was crystallised in the year AD 610 by a forty-year-
old camel trader turned visionary called Muhammad, the son
of Abdullah – a man who was, by all accounts, honest rather
than educated, and yet who came to be known as the last of
the prophets, the mouthpiece of God.

Down the centuries which separate us from the world which Muhammad knew, the Prophet and his Message have attracted fear, fervour and vitriolic bigotry. Even today, the heart of Islam – the message which he preached – is caricatured by the excesses, not by the excellence, of its followers. The Hezbollah in the Lebanon no more encapsulate the teachings of Muhammad than the paramilitary forces in Northern Ireland represent the way of Christ.

But what sober Islam teaches is more ambitious than the wildest dreams of any political extremists. It claims that God has spoken his last word to mankind, and that message, which supersedes both the Hebrew Bible and the New Testament, can be found only in the Qur'an, the literal, unadulterated word of God.

The way of the Prophet is based on five pillars: faith in the one God and his prophet Muhammad; prayer five times a day; the practice of almsgiving; fasting; and, finally, the holy pilgrimage to Mecca.

To the outsider, Islam is a bewildering faith of simplicity and paradox. In the cold light of historical analysis it is a faith in its middle ages – although its followers claim it is as old as time. It teaches a path of submission and of mercy, yet in practice it has often been imposed by the sword. But then it is not the only creed to have fallen into that trap.

For many non-Muslims of a Christian or Jewish background the story of Islam contains the surprise not of the exotic, but of the familiar. Adam, Eve, Noah, Abraham, Moses, John the Baptist and Jesus the son of Mary walk through the pages of the Qur'an. For Christians it remains an uncomfortable fact that Muslims have revered Jesus, the beloved of Allah, as consistently as Christians have reviled Muhammad. The most enduring distortion of Islam sets up Muhammad as a pseudo-Christ – an equation which mangles both Christianity and Islam. Any Muslim will insist that throughout the centuries of Islam, Muhammad, a man who was fond of milk and kind to all his ten wives, has been revered *only* for his humanity – anything else is blasphemy.

But that disclaimer is also misleading. Muhammad is the key to Islam. For the Muslim he is the most important man in the history of the past or the future.

What is so special about him? Was he more influenced than influencing? Why is it that Muslims believe *he*, the unlettered one, overshadows all other religious teachers? Did he really ride to heaven on a magical donkey/mule? Was he a hallucinator, a liar or a saint? Was he merely an efficient thief of ideas, or was he the preordained one, the pen of God?

The basic facts are these. Muhammad, literally 'he who is praised', was born in AD 570 into a merchant family. His was not a life of privilege. Abdullah, his father, died several months before Muhammad was born. His mother survived him by only six years. On one level, Muhammad's childhood is an unglamorous story of bereavement and dependence, survival and hard work. But however adamant Muslims are about Muhammad's ungarnished humanity, the earliest traditions about his life, contained in the Sira or biography of the Prophet, demonstrate an equally powerful conviction that from the earliest days of his childhood, spent in the care of Halima, his Bedouin wet nurse, he was the chosen one.

——————————— ∾ ———————————

I was suckled among the Banu Bakr, and while I was with a foster brother of mine behind our tents shepherding the lambs, two men in white raiment came to me with a gold basin full of snow. Then they seized me and opened up my belly, extracted my heart and split it; then they extracted a black drop from it and threw it away; then they washed my heart and my belly with that snow until they had cleansed them thoroughly.

——————————— ∾ ———————————

What does that story mean? Does it not elevate Muhammad to a superhuman plane? The theologian Professor Seyyed Hossein Nasr, of George Washington University, Washington DC, explains the story in this way. Snow, being white, symbolises purity. The angels use this snow to wash away the residues of sin which all mortals carry within themselves as a result of the Fall from the original state of perfection in Paradise. By washing the Prophet in this way, they make him free of sin.

To the non-Muslim, such a story, accepted at any but the most symbolic level, seems to undermine claims about Muhammad's mere humanity. But for the believer there is no problem – the story proves only the divinity of God. For Mashuq Ally, lecturer in Islamic studies at St David's College, Lampeter, these and similar stories are both humanly incredible and historically accurate.

The majority of Muslims, including himself, he says, would feel that the Sira is true – even those stories which appear to the outsider to be legend or miracle. There may be many disagreements even within the Muslim community about the history of the Prophet, but, by and large, he believes, much of the literature which is available is accurate.

The early Muslim artists who painted scenes from Muhammad's life showed the Prophet with a veil over his face. For the non-believing world the Prophet's personality is still shrouded in mystery. He is a half-remembered fear, rather than a person. To what extent is that ignorance inevitable? Is there much evidence about Muhammad the man? Kenneth Cracknell, a Methodist minister and formerly secretary of the committee for multi-faith issues at the British Council of Churches, says:

We know quite a lot about Muhammad, more in a sense than we know about Jesus. He was one of the most

10

extraordinary people that ever lived. He was a religious genius of exceptional proportions. He was a great general, a politician, a statesman, an unusual man in terms of his relations with women. The old detractors said he was over-sexed, but he actually liked women and cared for them. He must have had a considerable personal presence – a very remarkable human being.

That is a Christian view. For Nabilla Kawas, a Muslim and a civil engineer who is a research fellow at the City University, London, the force of Muhammad's personality lifts him out of history. He belongs to her world:

He is the example. In science, people first study theory and then see an experiment which is much easier for them to understand. The Prophet, peace be upon him, is like the experiment in front of my eyes. The way he led his life is an explanation of what Islam is. Because all those words could have more than one interpretation, the way he understood Qur'an and then led his life was an explanation of this. His wife once said, when they asked her how do you describe Muhammad, that his conduct was the Qur'an. In the human sense, I do not say I adore him, no, but I love God through him. I feel I know him, as if I have lived in his time, though there are nearly 1400 years between me and him – in fact not only him, his companions too. I feel I know these people, and I have the hope, if Allah give me his mercy, that I will meet them in heaven.

Over the centuries, others have been less enthusiastic. Muhammad has paid the price of his followers' success. When Islam began its victorious sweep beyond the Arabian peninsula, the character assassination began. Muhammad was the fiend Christian crusaders would keep at bay. Even in later years, he was the dark force of chaos threatening Christian Europe. Old prejudices die hard. Jabal Buaben, a Muslim from Ghana and author of a thesis on how Muhammad has been portrayed in Western scholarship, is convinced that they are still widespread.

Any book on Muhammad published in the West, he says, contains distortions which date back to the Middle Ages: such as accusations that Muhammad was violent, sensual, unable to perform miracles, epileptic, and that he copied his ideas and stories from the Biblical narratives.

Of all these charges, the one which hurts the most is the one which seems to non-Muslim eyes the most innocuous – the suggestion that Muhammad's religious ideas came at least in part from those around him. Is it feasible to isolate his religious ideas from the rest of history? Kenneth Cracknell believes that Muhammad was very much a product of his time and a product of history:

Remember he belonged to a very great city. Islam is not the religion of the desert. Mecca was a very great trading centre, the link between the West and the East – the camel trains came in and out – and Muhammad was a metropolitan man. He knew the stories both of Judaism and of Christianity, and he knew them mainly in heretical forms of which there were many by the sixth century. He certainly knew about Judaism because there were Jewish tribes living around Mecca. He had relatives, through his wife, who were Christians. The ideas of the Qur'an did not just come into his head. He was the product of what he knew at that time.

Mecca was more than just a great trading city linking Africa and Asia and Europe: it was also a religious centre of profound antiquity. At its centre lay the Ka'aba, the sanctuary first built, it was claimed, by Adam on his way out of Paradise, and rebuilt by Abraham and Ishmael. By Muhammad's time, Mecca and its religious heart were corrupted. The Ka'aba, the first temple to the one God, had become home to a different god for nearly every day of the year. It was a visual and aural cacophony of all the contemporary religions. There were altars to jinns, to nature spirits, to ancestor gods, the sun, the moon, fertility goddesses, Fate, Manaf, the lord of high places, Quzah, the god of storm, Nasr, Wadd and Astarte. The walls were covered with frescoes of religious stories, including paintings of Mary and Jesus.

Mecca was a crossroads of ideas as well as of merchandise. Muhammad the orphan would have had ample experience of both. After his mother died the six-year-old Muhammad had been entrusted to Abdul Muttalib, his grandfather, a revered and blind old man who spent every hour he could in the Ka'aba. But two years later, Abdul Muttalib died and Muhammad passed to the care of his uncle, Abu Talib, who initiated him into the world of commerce.

For many years, the young Muhammad travelled with his uncle's caravans of trading camels, but his future was not to be in trade. A Christian monk called Bahira was one of the first to notice that there was something special about the young Muhammad. As Sheikh Darsh, a Muslim scholar and lecturer, tells the story:

Muhammad's uncle took Muhammad with him at the age of twelve on a trading mission and they stopped at a Christian monastery as was their habit. When this Meccan group went in for hospitality Bahira asked, 'Is there anyone who's missing from among you?'

They replied, 'No, we are all here.'

Bahira said, 'I have seen certain signs. It indicates that there is another person with you.'

They said, 'There is a twelve-year-old boy outside.'

He said, 'That is the one I'm looking for.'

When Muhammad entered, he asked him to uncover his shoulder. Bahira had seen a physical indication on Muhammad's body which Muslims call the Seal – a white oval mark between the shoulder blades.

Bahira turned to Muhammad's uncle, Abu Talib, saying: 'Be careful – that young man is going to have a great future.'

But the great future was slow to materialise. Muhammad's adolescence and young adulthood were marked only by a reputation for probity. He came to be known as 'al-Amin' – the honest one – an unusual title for a Meccan whose city had become a byword for sharp practice, usury and extortion.

This reputation was instrumental in bringing about the most important alliance of Muhammad's life. The twice-widowed Khadija was so impressed by the young Muhammad's honesty and efficiency in carrying out trade on her behalf that through an intermediary she broached the possibility of marriage. Initially her family had doubts – she was after all nearly forty and he was only twenty-five. But Khadija had her way. The marriage, which was also a friendship, yielded six children.

We cannot be too sure what Muhammad looked like at this time. His cousin Ali describes him as being of average height, but broad-shouldered, inclined to lean forward as he walked, taking large strides. He had a longish face, according to Ali, with bushy eyebrows, curly hair and a thick beard – not an exceptional-looking man.

But he must have had some recognisable air of authority. When he was about thirty-five the Ka'aba was in need of repair. There was a great deal of wrangling over who should have the privilege of re-laying the sacred black stone, originally laid by Abraham. The four leading families of Mecca were each sure the honour should be theirs. There was stalemate, so it was resolved that the matter be settled by the first man to enter the courtyard of the Ka'aba. Muhammad was the first to enter. All the signs pointed to an insoluble problem, but with wisdom beyond his years Muhammad placed the sacred stone on his cloak and then instructed a representative of each of the four families to lift a corner of the cloak. All four lifted the cloak and Muhammad the peacemaker transferred the stone to its place of honour.

The simple wisdom of that action consolidated the respect felt for Muhammad by the Meccan community, but he did not capitalise on this. Increasingly, he began to withdraw from city life, to go up to the mountains to pray. And one night, known as the Night of Destiny, the silence of his meditation was broken.

Read: In the name of thy Lord Who createth,
Createth man from a clot.
Read: And thy Lord is the Most Bounteous,
Who teacheth by the pen,
Teacheth man that which he knew not.

Sura: 96:1–5, The Clot

These are the first words of the Qur'an, dictated, Muslims believe, by the Archangel Gabriel. Dr Abdel-Haleem of London University recounts the story:

Muhammad was sitting contemplating in a cave in the night on Mount Hira, when he was approached by an angel who said to him, 'Read.' And he said, 'I cannot read.' So the angel shook him and repeated the question again. And the third time he said to him the words quoted above.

This was Muhammad's first experience of revelation. After that, we have recordings of what actually happened, because it took place in the full light of day with his companions around him. Muhammad would all of a sudden fall silent, his face would grow red and perspire even on cold days, and they said that if you were near him you would hear something like humming around his face. This would last for a few moments, and then, as it left him, Muhammad would recite new verses of the Qur'an.

These states of the revelation would simply descend on him. He could not invite them. He could not avert them. They might happen while he was making a speech, while he was sitting, even while he was riding his camel. He commanded his scribes to record the verses of the Qur'an he recited after such a revelation. Stylistically the revelations are very different from Muhammad's own recorded words – as different as the great passages of Shakespeare compared with the popular press.

Orthodox Muslim tradition maintains that Muhammad was *ummi*, that is Arabic for illiterate, an unlikely handicap for a successful merchant let alone a would-be messenger of God. But Gai Eaton, an Islamic convert and lecturer at the London mosque in Regent's Park, believes, on the contrary, that it was an essential qualification. He says that Muhammad was called *ummi* – but although *ummi* is often translated as illiterate it also means untouched by profane knowledge, untouched by knowledge from any source other than God. In other words, Muhammad was a blank page upon which the divine pen could write. Muslim pride in the illiteracy of Muhammad is crucial. It guarantees that the word is not his but God's.

At first Muhammad told only Khadija about what had happened on Mount Hira. She comforted and encouraged him. She was his first convert. He shared the revelation about the oneness of God with other members of his immediate family, but it was three years before he preached his first public sermon to a meeting of his extended family.

His message was not taken seriously, but Muhammad continued to recite his revelations and a small group of followers dedicated themselves to memorising every word he spoke while receiving them. Opposition to him began to mount. Then as now the Prophet was accused of plagiarism, an understandable charge when so many of the stories of the Qur'an seem influenced either by the Hebrew Bible or by the Gospels. But according to Jabal Buaben, a Muslim scholar from Ghana, familiar content should be a vindication, not an indictment, of the divine nature of the Qur'an:

If God is one – and Christians and Jews believe it so – and if He is the source of revelation, what prevents God from revealing to Muhammad what he has revealed to Jesus, to Moses and to others? It was up to God to reveal whatever he wanted to reveal and therefore it was not a matter of copying. It is true – there is some historical evidence – that Muhammad met quite a few scholars. His first wife's uncle, called Waraqa bin Alfal, was supposed to be learned in the Scriptures. Khadija took Muhammad to see her uncle who said that it was unfortunate that he was not going to live for long since he would have protected Muhammad. Waraqa died soon after that, shortly after Muhammad received his first revelation. However, some scholars still suggest that Waraqa might have taught Muhammad some of the Bible stories.

The Qur'an refutes such a suggestion. It says that Muhammad was not taught by anybody – his words were God's own revelation. Islam is not preoccupied with identifying the many roots its stories share with other faiths; its only concern is the single flower of revelation, which is Islam.

Coincidence of belief is collaborative, not damaging, proof. As Professor Nasr explains it:

Muslims believe that no prophet owes anything to anyone except to God. God revealed Islam in the Arabian milieu, within the climate of the Abrahamic Semitic monotheisms, and therefore the same realities and truths which he had revealed in one way or another in Judaism and Christianity, he revealed in still another way in the Qur'an. So there are certain stories in the Old Testament which are also accepted by Christians, and which appear in the Qur'an – sometimes the same, sometimes different. It is the same sacred history, not taken by the Prophet and copied or plagiarised or heard from some people in Mecca and Medina and then put into a new form, but revealed to him by God as sacred history for a new religion.

For Muslims acceptance of the prophets and patriarchs of Judaism and Christianity is not an optional extra: believing in the Torah of Moses, in many of the stories of Judaism and Christianity, is part of the first pillar of Islam. As Dr Abdel-Haleem says, one cannot be a Muslim without believing in the earlier Scriptures and the earlier prophets of whom

Muhammad was the last. The Qur'an confirms the Scriptures that have come before it and stands as guardian over them.

Down the years in the non-Muslim world, there has been a consistent emphasis on what Muslims do *not* believe in rather than on what they do. Medieval crusaders fighting for their faith far from home would have been surprised had they realised the simple truth that Mary, the mother of Jesus, is mentioned more often in the Qur'an than in the Gospels. For the Muslim, the Qur'an as revealed to Muhammad, the illiterate one, completes and perfects the beliefs which came before.

As Mashuq Ally says:

> The Prophet Muhammad continues the message of all the prophets from the time of Adam – Adam being the first prophet in Islam. The revelation which Muhammad received, which is embodied in the Qur'an, brings together and encapsulates everything that had gone before. The Qur'an can be seen as concerned with three things: beliefs, values and norms. To express them it draws on history, and therefore you find the Qur'an very much concerned with the history of those who believe in the revealed word, such as the Christians and the Jews, to underpin those beliefs and values which it feels to be universal and eternal and applicable to all time.
>
> The actions of Muhammad, which are embodied in what is called the Sunna or Hadith literature – these are the sayings and practices of the Prophet Muhammad – is distinct from the revelation, but has the sanction of revelation. It has the sanction of revelation because Muhammad becomes the first interpreter of the Qur'an, just as Jesus was the interpreter of the revelation that he was given, and Moses too. The Prophet Muhammad

becomes a beacon light, the life example of the revealed
word.

But there are times when Islam and Christianity talk at
cross purposes. A Muslim will analyse and interpret the
Qur'an, but he will not doubt it. The Christian preoccupa-
tion with dissecting biblical texts and comparing differing
versions has no place in Muslim tradition. So how has the
Qur'an achieved such an inviolable status?

Kenneth Cracknell explains that this is because the Qur'an
came into existence in a much more concrete way than the
New Testament:

> The New Testament, which was written years after
> Jesus's death, contains four different versions of the
> same story – there is no final version. The words of the
> Qur'an were recited. Sometimes they were written
> down on bits of parchment and clay or even the shoul-
> der blades of camels, but on the whole they just
> remained in people's hearts. The third Caliph Othman
> decided that there should be an authentic version, and
> he arranged for it to be made by a man called Said Ibn
> T'abit. Othman made public the results of this, and had
> all the other Qur'ans which had been written destroyed
> so that only one form of the Qur'an exists. There are no
> variant readings – everybody has the same text. Other
> people also collected sayings which were not part of the
> Qur'an, but traditions – the Hadith – of what the
> Prophet said. There are several collections of the
> Hadith which are considered authoritative by Muslims.

This is a source of strength, but it is not a guarantee of simplicity. The Qur'an will be as deep as the understanding of its

readers. It contains no doubts but it does have its secrets. Syed Ali Ashraf, the director of the Islamic Academy in Cambridge, says that there are two types of meanings in the Qur'an: one explicit, the other hidden. But the Qur'an contains a warning against those who want to create mischief and disturbance by trying to give it meanings of their own. Only Allah and those he has chosen understand the deeper meanings. These people have deep intuitive understanding because of their obedience to the Prophet and their knowledge – the knowledge given to them by God himself. But there are very very few of them, and some of these meanings they never disclose.

A tradition of mysticism lies at the core of Islam. In the year AD 619 Muhammad experienced the pain of bereavement. Khadija, his first wife and his most loyal supporter, died. A few months later Abu Talib, his uncle and guardian, also died. This year of grief was to be a preparation for the greatest of Muhammad's religious experiences – the *miraj*, or the Night Ride, of Muhammad the apostle of Islam, to the holy city of Jerusalem, on a flying donkey-mule, and his ascent from the Temple of Solomon to the gates of heaven.

——————————————— ⌣ ———————————————

The apostle said: 'While I was sleeping Gabriel came and stirred me with his foot. I sat up but saw nothing and lay down again. He came a second time and stirred me with his foot. I sat up but saw nothing and lay down again. He came to me the third time and stirred me with his foot. I sat up and he took hold of my arm and I stood beside him and he brought me out to the door of the mosque and there was a white animal, half mule, half donkey, with wings on its sides with which it propelled its feet, putting down each forefoot at the limit of its sight and he mounted me on it. Then he went out with me keeping close to me.'

The apostle and Gabriel went their way until they arrived at the temple at Jerusalem. There he found Abraham, Moses, and Jesus among a company of the prophets. The apostle acted as their imam in prayer.

The apostle said, 'After the completion of my business in Jerusalem a ladder was brought to me finer than any I have ever seen. It was that to which the dying man looks when death approaches. My companion mounted it with me until we came to one of the gates of heaven called the Gate of the Watchers. An angel called Isma'il was in charge of it, and under his command were twelve thousand angels each of them having twelve thousand angels under his command. When Gabriel brought me in, Isma'il asked who I was, and when he was told that I was Muhammad he asked if I had been given a mission, and on being assured of this he wished me well.

꙳

From the gates of heaven, Muhammad ascended through all the spheres of creation. He met again the prophets he had prayed with in Jerusalem. Abraham, he later mentioned, looked rather like himself. Moses was thin and Jesus the son of Mary was covered with freckles. Muhammad progressed through all the heavens until he came into the presence of Allah, the Compassionate, the Uncreated One, the only God. There, beyond time and space, in a world only incredible because we are bound by time and space, Muhammad worshipped his Lord.

The Night Ride is a story with two meanings, as Professor Nasr explains. This event, he says, is, according to traditional Islamic doctrine, both inward and outward. All Muslims, if they are pious and virtuous, can have this so-called inner or spiritual ascension towards God. But the Prophet was given the special privilege of experiencing this with the whole of his being, including the spiritual and the physical.

Muslims will happily agree that elements of the story are mythical – like Buraq, the magical human-faced donkey-mule. But for believers, the story's mythical elements do not detract from its reality. Syed Ali Ashraf argues that it is not legend but truth. Muhammad actually went to the throne of God, met God and talked to Him. When asked whether it was just a journey of the mind or a physical journey Ashraf says that we must try to understand what the body is. What happens when a man is dead? There is a spirit – but what happens to the body? What is matter? According to modern science, matter can be transformed into light; so, if the body can be transformed into light, the body can travel anywhere.

And Professor Nasr points out that the theology of the Night Ride was not without precedent. According to the traditional understanding of the Resurrection, not certain modern interpretations, on Easter Sunday the body of Christ rose from the dead and was taken to heaven. In all Abrahamic religions the body is not something pejorative and negative, but is integrated in the final experience of man. That is why Judaism, Christianity and Islam all believe in the resurrection of the body as well as of the soul. So the Prophet's Night Ride can be compared to Christ's Resurrection, and also, according at least to Catholic doctrine, to the Assumption of the Virgin. These comparisons are useful because they bring out certain very profound relationships between the various religions.

But in whatever way Muhammad's Night Ride is understood, it had a very practical outcome. It was during Muhammad's experience of the presence of God that the framework of prayer which holds every Muslim's belief was agreed upon. God wanted men to pray fifty times a day – Muhammad bargained on mankind's behalf and a less demanding timetable of five daily prayers was agreed on.

The Night Ride was a turning point in Muhammad's life.

He began gaining converts on a far larger scale. Success inevitably brought persecution and in AD 622 Muhammad fled from Mecca to Medina. This journey, known as the *Hijira*, came to be recognised as Year 1 of the new calendar. For the next eight years Muhammad was forced into the rôle of warrior. And then, in AD 630, he re-entered Mecca and cleared the Ka'aba of all its idols, leaving only Abraham's black stone. Mecca was now sacred to the one God alone.

For the two remaining years of Muhammad's life he waged war against local Arab pagan beliefs. His successors would have to face greater battles because of a prophet from Nazareth, believed by Muslims to share in Muhammad's mission. As Mashuq Ally says, for Islam, the mission of Jesus Christ and the mission of Muhammad is one and the same. The mission of all the prophets of Islam, which include Abraham and Moses, is to invite human beings to believe in one God. This was the primary function of Muhammad, as well as of Jesus Christ. The difference between Islam and Christianity is that, for the Muslim, Jesus Christ was a human being with a mission, while for the Christian, he is the Son of God or God on earth.

That difference has brought many believers in the one God to a bloody and early death. The point at issue is important, but it is not as simple as a straightforward rivalry between Jesus and Muhammad. Gai Eaton says that the comparison is sometimes made between the Qur'an on the one hand, and Jesus as seen by Christians on the other. In the one case, the divine word becomes book, becomes writing. In the other, the divine word becomes man, becomes flesh. And therefore the role of Muhammad – this is an idea that several Westerners have put forward – is comparable to that of the Virgin Mary: he gives birth to the book in a sense, as she gave birth to Jesus. Another interesting contrast which has been made is that the Christian message is believed because of the

splendour of the messenger, that is of Jesus, while Muhammad is revered because of the splendour of the message.

Christianity has been part of the story of Islam from its
earliest days. Jesus and his message were of the greatest
importance to Muhammad. But, as Kenneth Cracknell says,
Islam's relationship to Christianity has been very compli-
cated right from the beginning. In the Qur'an there is one
verse which says: 'It shall be when you tell this story of Islam
to the monks, that their eyes will fill with tears. They will
weep with joy.' But in other places Muhammad is very
strongly against Christians, largely for changing the Scriptures. Jesus is important to Islam. In the Qur'an he is called
Isa, and there is a Qur'anic verse which says that in the last
day, Jesus will point to the Christians and he will say, 'I did
not tell you this, I did not tell you that I was God's son. You
are mistaken.'

In the course of history, tears have given way to fears.
Islam's survival and success provoked hostility, charges of
heresy and accusations of inhumanity. As Islam persisted,
Christians, from about the eleventh century AD, began to
write books, mostly in Latin and later on in vernacular lan-
guages, campaigning against Islam. But, as Professor Nasr
points out, since in Christianity the most central and important figure was Christ, Christians thought that in attacking
Islam the best tactic would be to concentrate on the Prophet.
Thus Muhammad became the main target for these attacks
which appeared throughout Europe and have survived into
the twentieth century.

Such attacks always focused on the personality of the
Prophet, and furthered a misconception of his function and
his importance. They spread the idea that the Prophet was an
impostor and that he was not an unworldly person – rather he
had lived fully in the world and was married (and had more
than one wife). The fact that he was the leader of men, that he

was a judge, that he was the ruler of a community, was held against him, because it was juxtaposed to the ideal of Christ who said 'My kingdom is not of this world', and who represented perfect sanctity, perfect spirituality. But Christ never married, nor had to deal with the darker side of human nature, and therefore the question of turning the other cheek became the law for the saints who were produced within the Christian community. The Prophet of Islam was seen as an imperfect and much too human figure in comparison with the divine figure of Christ.

The divinity of Christ will always be unacceptable to Muslims, but the humanity of their Prophet, the orphan of Mecca whose heart was washed in snow, is something they are willing to share. According to Kenneth Cracknell:

God is Allah. There are some people who say Allah was one of the many gods of Mecca. Not so: Allah is actually the Arabic word for God.

When Muhammad received his earliest revelations, he took them to a nephew of his wife who was Jewish and said, 'What do you make of these?'

And this Jew said to him, 'These are the words given to Moses, this is the same story, this is the living God. No question but that this is the God of Abraham.'

All three faiths, Jewish, Christian, Muslim, are what we call Abrahamic faiths – same faith, same God.

2

A Lesson from the Daughter of a Gazelle

'There is no god but God and Muhammad is his Prophet.'

Sura 2:255, The Cow and *Sura 48:29, Victory*

The Qur'an is a complex book, asking to be read on many levels. It not only teaches, but it also assumes that its readers and reciters will be already familiar with the stories used and characters referred to. Above all the Qur'an employs rich allusive technique. In style it is set apart from the historical flavour of large parts of the Hebrew bible or the direct narrative simplicity of the Gospels.

For Muslims, Muhammad is the greatest messenger of God, the seal of the prophets. Similarly the Qur'an is seen as God's final word to mankind. The stories it contains do not need to be complete in every detail – the Qur'an is not an encyclopaedia. But what is important is the final insight or twist given to a well-known story. This is the element which separates the contents of the Qur'an from all preceding sources, religious or traditional.

Nowhere is this more evident than in the Qur'anic handling of Solomon and the Queen of Sheba. The Qur'an assumes its readers will be familiar with the historical Solomon, the shrewd horse-dealing king of Israel, famed for his wisdom and his wives. Solomon's reputation as the great temple builder and pioneering trader had assured him a place in the popular traditions common to both the lands of Israel and Arabia.

As the centuries had passed Solomon had become a byword for ingenious fairness – a paragon of justice to be copied by all rulers. And the years had given Solomon other skills as well. He could, it was believed, speak the language of birds and employed them as information carriers and gatherers – a feathered and less menacing prototype of the secret services. Solomon is also associated with the romance of courtly love. In the Judaeo-Christian tradition he is fancifully credited with authorship of the Song of Songs and his name is inextricably linked with a woman of several names or none – the Queen of Sheba.

The first book of Kings describes how the Queen of Sheba, fascinated by the accounts she had heard of Solomon's knowledge of God, made the journey to Jerusalem to meet him. She wanted to probe his understanding of the divine. This alone, the Bible says, was the motive for her journey. She arrived in Jerusalem with camels laden with spices, gold and precious stones. She cross-examined Solomon and was shown the daily routine of the court including the animals set aside to be sacrificed as burnt offerings in the temple.

This impressed her deeply. She told Solomon that his wealth of wisdom exceeded the rumours she had heard and added that God must love Israel with a deep love to give the people such a righteous and just king. And blessing the God of Israel the Queen lavished gifts on Solomon and his court. Never, before or after, observed the writer of the Book of Kings, had such a quantity of spices been seen in Jerusalem. Solomon in return plied the queen with whatever riches she wanted and more besides. Thus laden, the Queen of Sheba, still nameless, walks out of the Bible and back to her own country.

But the story of the mysterious queen captured people's imaginations. The Ethiopians claimed her. They said that before leaving Jerusalem the Queen, who was called Makeda, became one of Solomon's wives, and their son Menelik grew to be the progenitor of the ruling house of Ethiopia.

More often and more probably the Queen was claimed as the ruler of the merchant traders of Saba or Sheba – a region corresponding to modern Yemen – whose people were destined to become early converts to Islam. Certainly stories about Solomon and the Queen of Sheba were part of the pre-Qur'anic oral tradition of Arabia. It was generally assumed that Solomon and the Queen of Sheba were married and that the Queen's name was Bilquis. That name gives a further clue to her home and significance. The ruins of the ancient Sabean capital Mariaba, modern Mareb, contain a massive circular wall which was part of the temple dedicated to one of the pantheon of Babylonian deities, the goddess Bilquis.

Arabian folk tales speak of both Solomon and Bilquis as commanding 'jinn' or spirits. Bilquis is firmly rooted in the paganism of the ancient Yemen. She is described as having a royal human father but a jinn mother who was captured when she had assumed the shape of a gazelle. Bilquis bore the marks of her strange background throughout her life – her legs were covered with the hair you would expect to find not on a princess but on a gazelle.

The Arabian stories describe how Solomon heard of the Queen's power and paganism from one of his bird spies and decided to arrange a test for her. With this in mind he transported her throne from Mariaba to Jerusalem and had it subtly altered as part of his plan to see whether she was guided by truth and so would be able to recognise it in its changed guise. He also made sure that she would be received in a room paved with glass so that he would be able to find out whether the rumours about the gazelle hair on her legs were true. The tale ends happily. Bilquis is unable to recognise her own throne so exchanges belief in the false gods who have guided her wrongly for submission to the one God. Her legs are discovered to be hairy so Solomon orders hair removal treatment before marrying her.

Some of the elements of this tradition are to be found in the Qur'an, but only the most important ones. Bilquis, the daughter of a gazelle, is not depicted as a romantic heroine or a semi-divine being. She is used as a lesson in the oneness of God and the unreliability of the senses.

Her failure to recognise her own throne is proof that the gods she worships are not gods at all. Her inability to see through the ruse of the glass floor illustrates the illusions which can be perpetrated by the senses. In the Qur'an the queen bares her legs, assuming she is about to cross a hall of water. There is no mention of hairy legs or marriage with Solomon. The story points to something much more important. When the queen recognises she has been duped by the glass floor, she cries out, 'My Lord! Lo! I have wronged myself, and I surrender with Solomon unto Allah, the Lord of the Worlds.' (*Sura 27:44, The Ant*)

For the powerful and the weak, for queens and commoners, Islam is the faith of submission to the one God. It is a faith of actions not rarefied debate. The journey of faith that is Islam requires that everything but God should be questioned. The twentieth century has many floors of glass. Every Muslim must be prepared for a journey more arduous than the cameltrain between Bilquis' Sheba and Solomon's Jerusalem. And for guidance on that journey the believer must place his faith not in false gods but in the five pillars of Islam.

It is typical of the forthrightness of Islam that these pillars are not abstruse points which can be grasped only by the theologically learned. The pillars – profession of faith, worship, almsgiving, fasting and pilgrimage – are all practices which can be undertaken by every believer.

The story of the gazelle's daughter points to the paramount importance of the first pillar, the *shahada* (in Urdu *kalma*) or profession of faith, which alone is the motive for the other four pillars. 'There is no god but God,' may not sound revolutionary to modern Western ears, long accustomed as they are to the dominance of the three Abrahamic faiths in the religious world, but the story of Bilquis, half jinn, half human, is a reminder that in seventh century Arabia Muhammad's insistence on such stark monotheism was, in a very literal sense, shocking. Muhammad left behind a legacy which challenged and still challenges the intricate web of belief and unquestioned half belief which for many, from the seventh century to the twentieth century, is the nearest they come to faith. Bilquis had power, wealth and false religious belief. None of these counts for anything when weighed against the first pillar of Islam. For the Muslim, Muhammad, the mouthpiece of God, teaches a way of life which can neither compromise with the gods of the past nor deify the power and materialism of the present.

The *shahada* is recited by every new convert to Islam. It is repeated every time Muslims gather to pray. It should not be surprising then that *shirk*, or polytheism, is the greatest sin any Muslim can commit and the only one which God the all-forgiving will not readily forgive. Indeed, the most loathed critics of Islam are those who question its monotheism.

The Qur'an speaks of angels, Iblis or Satan, the fallen one, and the jinn. It must be remembered Islam did not evolve in a religious vacuum. Angels and fallen angels – neither gods nor men – play their part in the drama of the fight for men's souls as they do in many other religious traditions, but this does not compromise the Qur'an's monotheism.

The second Sura of the Qur'an clearly sets out the role of the angels. From the earliest times they have been sent down to earth as clear signs to mankind.

Say (O Muhammad, to mankind): Who is an enemy to Gabriel! For he it is who hath revealed (this Scripture) to thy heart by Allah's leave, confirming that which was (revealed) before it, and a guidance and glad tidings to believers;

Who is an enemy to Allah, and His angels and His messengers, and Gabriel and Michael! Then, lo! Allah (Himself) is an enemy to the disbelievers.

Sura 2:97 & 98, The Cow

For the Muslim, faith in angels is not an optional extra – it is part of his or her faith in God. Whoever is an enemy of the angels is no true believer.

The Qur'an speaks of two orders of angels, which is at least simpler than the nine hierarchies of angels described by the Christian theologian Dionysius the Areopagite (*c*.500). Foremost among the angels of Islam is Jibra'il – more recognisable as Gabriel to Christians and Jews. Jibra'il plays a pivotal part in the spread of Islam. His is the voice which reveals to Muhammad on the Night of Destiny that he had been chosen as the messenger of God. As Muhammad returns home from the cave of revelation on Mount Hira he looks up to the sky and, wherever he looks, he sees Jibra'il in the form of a man standing astride the horizon.

Ten years later, Jibra'il appears to Muhammad again. This time he is his guide on the *miraj* or Night Ride to Heaven and introduces the Prophet to the teachers of the will of God who have gone before him. He accompanies Muhammad through all the heavens until they approach the presence of God. Jibra'il, for all his might as an angel, has to withdraw – his eyes cannot bear the brilliant light of the throne of God. Muhammad too closes his eyes for fear of blindness but then he finds he can look upon God with the eyes of his heart.

Jibra'il, the angel of revelation, is therefore a reminder that simple human faith can draw the believer nearer to God than any physical or intellectual power. In Muslim tradition Jibra'il is spoken of as a shining figure whose saffron hair is as bright as the stars. His greatest glory is a distinctive mark between his eyes – it is an inscription of the words of the *shahada* 'There is no god but God and Muhammad is his Prophet.'

Jibra'il's fellow angels include Mika'il (Michael), the Angel of Providence, Israfil, the Angel of the Trumpet of Doom, and Azra'il, the Angel of Death. The second order of angels are less glorious. They include Ridwan, the Chamberlain of Paradise, Malik, the Chamberlain of Hell and Munkar and Makir, the recording angels who interrogate the dead.

The fallen angels, led by Iblis or Satan, with Babylon's two evil angels, Harut and Marut, remind Muslim believers that it is always possible to fall from grace. In Muslim, as in Christian and Jewish tradition, the fallen angels are dedicated to misleading mankind. In Christian tradition Lucifer becomes Satan because his pride will not let him worship God. In the Qur'an the reason for the angelic fall is subtly changed – mankind holds centre stage.

The Qur'an describes the creation of man when God moulded the first man out of the lowliest of all substances, not air, fire or water, but mud. When God completed his work he breathed his spirit into the moulded mud and it became man. All the angels bowed down before the new creation except one – Iblis.

And the jinn did We create aforetime of essential fire.
And (remember) when thy Lord said unto the angels:
  Lo! I am creating a mortal out of potter's clay of
  black mud altered,
So, when I have made him and have breathed into
  him of My Spirit, do ye fall down, prostrating
  yourselves unto him.
So the angels fell prostrate, all of them together
Save Iblis. He refused to be among the prostrate.
HE said: O Iblis! What aileth thee that thou art not
  among the prostrate?
He said: I am not one to prostrate myself unto a
  mortal whom Thou hast created out of potter's clay
  of black mud altered!
HE said: Then go thou forth from hence, for lo! thou
  art outcast.
And lo! the curse shall be upon thee till the Day of
  Judgement.
He said: My Lord! Reprieve me till the day when
  they are raised.
HE said: Then lo! thou art of those reprieved
Till the Day of appointed time.
He said: My Lord! Because Thou hast sent me astray,
  I verily shall adorn the path of error for them in the
  earth, and shall mislead them every one,
Save such of them as are Thy perfectly devoted
  slaves.
HE said: This is a right course incumbent upon Me:
Lo! as for My slaves, thou hast no power over any of
  them save such of the froward as follow thee,
And lo! for all such, hell will be the promised place.

Sura 15:27–43, Al-Hijr

Iblis, who could not see that the spirit of God should be revered no matter where it resides, would never do homage to a mortal born of mud. From that moment on Iblis was cursed and he and his followers tempt the faithful and lead the faithless away from God.

Angels and fallen angels no more invalidate the monotheism of Islam than they do the monotheism of Judaism and Christianity. At first glance, the fire-born jinn may seem more problematic but they too are far from rival gods. They are spirits set well below the lowest of the angels. They can inspire, mislead or possess men. They were created by God and are subordinate to him. Some are good and some are not. Their inclusion in the Qur'an should not be seen as an embarrassment. They are constant reminders that man is not the centre of God's universe, God is the centre of man's. The universe has many secrets and purposes which are still hidden. Mankind has no reason to assume it is the limit of God's creative powers.

In a way the jinn have become the buttresses of Islam's monotheism. Their existence, imperfectly understood, is described as one of the reasons why the people of pre-Islamic Mecca worshipped goddesses like Al-hat, Al-Uzzah and Al-Manat and other deities who were either the fruits of man's imagination or, at best, bungled attempts at identifying spirits or natural forces higher and stronger than humans but still created by the one God.

Every Muslim knows that he or she lives in a world larger than that which can be perceived by the senses. Every Muslim knows that their lifespan on earth is only part of their life. By submitting to the one God and reciting the *shahada* they acknowledge that they belong to an immeasurably great creation. The jinn and the angels, faithful and fallen, are one way of beginning to grasp that there are concepts beyond the understanding of the human mind.

In the folklore of Islam, Azra'il, the angel of death, is said to be so great that he can toss the world in his hands as easily as men and women can jangle loose change in their pockets. He lives enthroned in the Sixth Heaven, his body covered by thousands upon thousands of eyes. The lifespan of each creature is determined before his birth and whenever one of Azra'il's eyes blink, a human soul dies.

For the faithful believer there should be nothing daunting about living in a world larger than life. Death should be seen as an awakening, not as a meaningless theft of life.

Islam has no doubts about the afterlife. If anything it is more real than this life. Hopes for the afterlife are expressed with verve and exuberance. There will be no old women in Paradise, the Prophet is supposed to have remarked. They will not be excluded but they will all be made young and beautiful as they enter its gates! Many pleasures await the 'Companions of the Light' – the blessed.

───────────────── ᗢ ─────────────────

And the foremost in the race, the foremost in the
  race:
Those are they who will be brought nigh
In gardens of delight;
A multitude of those of old
And a few of those of later time.
On lined couches,
Reclining therein face to face.
There wait on them immortal youths
With bowls and ewers and a cup from a pure spring
Wherefrom they get no aching of the head nor any
  madness,
And fruit that they prefer
And flesh of fowls that they desire.
And (there are) fair ones with wide, lovely eyes,
Like unto hidden pearls,

Reward for what they used to do.
They hear they no vain speaking nor recrimination
(Naught) but the saying: Peace, (and again) Peace.
And those on the right hand; what of those on the
  right hand?
Among thornless lote-trees
And clustered plantains,
And spreading shade,
And water gushing,
And fruit in plenty
Neither out of reach nor yet forbidden,
And raised couches;
Lo! We have created them a (new) creation
And made them virgins,
Lovers, friends,
For those on the right hand;

Sura 56:10-38, The Event

For many non-Muslims there is something disturbingly sensual about the Islamic concept of Paradise. At the simplest level it is depicted as a garden of delights where the virtuous can enjoy all the pleasures abstained from in life. They can recline on sumptuous couches and eat and drink without fear of intoxication attended by wide-eyed virgins who manage to be both chaste and amorous at the same time. The gardens of Moorish Spain, the recurring garden designs woven into Eastern carpets, show how strongly the Qur'anic description of an ideal garden world – well watered and shaded by thornless trees – inspired the Muslim imagination.

Paradise, the Muslim mystics explain, rewards the faithful for their sacrifices on earth. But the golden pavilions and crystal streams are only the first step in the journey of the afterlife. Before long the blessed are summoned to the presence of God. That call marks a turning point in the afterlife.

All the pleasures of the garden of delight will seem as nothing when compared to this summons. Having decked themselves in their finest clothes and jewels, the believers will leave the pavilions allocated to them and set out once again on the journey towards the one God and the beginning of all life.

The believers will be led to the Garden of Eden. Life, death and afterlife have formed a perfect circle. There the faithful will have life with an unimaginable fullness. Beneath the trees of Eden they will sit on jewel-encrusted thrones. They will eat food, finer than they have ever tasted before. They will drink the finests liquids out of vessels made from pearl. They will be perfumed and clothed beyond the richness of dreams. And in the garden each will have his place according to his closeness with God.

Finally, they will hear the voice of God asking if their hearts long for anything else and telling them of the ultimate delight which will outshine all others. Deep in the Garden of Eden, not a place of disgrace, the faithful believers will be drawn into the presence of the one God who made the first man at the beginning of time and beckons each believer through life, with all its deceptive senses and its suffering, through the joys of the afterlife, to full life in Him.

Every word of the Qur'an, all its characters – human, spirits and angels – lead to this final unity. Many men and women, like the daughter of the gazelle, will be beguiled by the artifice of the world. But if they walk in the path of the Prophet, guided by the profession of faith which is the first pillar of Islam, they will be able to see through the worthless and unreal and they will be able to say with Bilquis, 'My Lord, I have wronged myself, and I surrender . . . unto Allah, the Lord of the Worlds.' (*Sura 27:44, The Ant*)

3

A Voice from the Halls
of Diamond and Stone

Establish worship at the going down of the sun until the
dark of night, and (the recital of) the Qur'an at dawn
. . . the Qur'an at dawn is ever witnessed. . . .

And say: Praise be to Allah, who hath not taken unto
Himself a son, and Who hath no partner in the Sovereignty, nor hath He any protecting friend through
dependence. And magnify Him with all Magnificence.

Sura 17:78 & 111, The Children of Israel

There is one practice which more than any other sums up for
non-Muslims the strength of Islam. It is *salat* or worship, the
duty to pray five times every day, which joins Muslims all
over the world as they kneel turning their bodies towards
Mecca and their hearts towards God.

Salat (in Urdu *namaz*), the prayer of the faithful, is the second pillar of Islam. It weaves through the life of every Muslim believer. It offers not only an alternative timetable for
the day – mankind is made for more than working, eating and
sleeping – but also an alternative framework of priorities. It
is the thread which binds together all believers whether they
are masters of mysticism or possessors of the most simple,
instinctive, childlike faith.

In Islam, prayer is emphatically not only for the professionally religious. It should come as no surprise then to find that lessons in worship can be drawn from almost every part of Muslim culture. Prayer crops up in the most unlikely places – even in fairy tales as the story of Zobeide the prudent, tradeswoman of Baghdad, demonstrates.

Zobeide can be found in the collection of Arabian stories known to generations of non-Muslim children as *The Book of A Thousand and One Arabian Nights*, tales first told, it is claimed, by a sultan's wife to put off the date of her execution. In the end we are told the stories won her not only a reprieve but also a pardon.

The story of Zobeide's adventures, which was part of this life-saving recital, contains many of the elements of classic folktale. There are malevolent elder sisters, miraculous transformations and winged serpents, but there are other messages as well which have nothing to do with fantasy.

Zobeide, the story goes, was an orphan but a resourceful one. Her elder sisters made disastrous marriages and watched helpless as their husbands frittered away their inheritances. Zobeide was more canny. She went into business as a silkworm grower and her business prospered.

Able to support herself and her less shrewd sisters quite comfortably, Zobeide decided to expand her entrepreneurial skills. Loading up with stock from Baghdad she set sail from Balsora in her own merchant vessel. She set her course for the Indies and twenty days out of the Persian Gulf she made landfall in a promisingly built-up looking harbour.

Eager to do trade, Zobeide was the first to disembark. She made her way through the town's strangely silent streets, her curiosity turning to fear as she realised that the first group of men she approached were no longer alive but were turned to stone. Pressing on to the merchants' quarter, she saw all the shops were shut – with no sound of haggling coming from behind the closed doors. Not a single plume of smoke rose from any of the chimneys.

Finally Zobeide found herself on the steps of an imposing palace. She made her way past the stone guards and cautiously progressed from room to room. In the palace she saw riches beyond the wildest dreams of the most acquisitive merchant – even the window shutters were made of gold and the throne room was ablaze with light caught and refracted in a perfect diamond as large as an ostrich egg.

Before long she was hopelessly lost in the treasure-strewn maze. Meanwhile it was growing dark. There was nothing else for it – Zobeide settled down to sleep in the deserted throne room.

At midnight she awoke and heard at some distance the sound of a man praying. The familiar cadences of the Qur'an being recited gave her courage and reminded her of home. She made her way to the room where the sound of praise was coming from. With great daring, she pushed the door ajar and there to her delight her eyes met an accustomed sight, far removed from the horror of the petrified city. What she saw was and is commonplace anywhere in the Muslim world. She saw a young man praying on a prayer mat, reciting verses from the Qur'an which was lying open on a stand in front of him. In front of the man was a niche pointing in the direction of Mecca.

Zobeide entered the room and standing in front of the niche made her prayer too. The young man was amazed to see another living creature and overjoyed to meet another believer. Immediately he began to tell her the sorry story of his doomed, treasure-laden city. He was, he explained, the only son of the royal house of the cursed kingdom. All his family, all his fellow countrymen, had been turned into stone. They had been fire worshippers dedicated to the idol Nardoun. He alone in all the country had been a true believer, taught faith in his childhood by a Muslim governess. Some three years previously God had called the people of his kingdom to abjure Nardoun and instead worship the one, true God. The people had ignored that call. Confident in their wealth, they saw no need to worship God. They turned their hearts to stone and persisted in the praise of Nardoun. Before long, their bodies had turned to stone as well.

Having told his story and expressed his delight at meeting another believer, the prince eagerly accepted Zobeide's invitation to return with her to Baghdad and exchange his solitary life for the brotherhood of faith.

All does not run completely smoothly. Other adventures await Zobeide but her encounter with the solitary prince is the kernel of her story which makes it more than a fairy tale. Down the centuries Zobeide and her prince have taught their readers some essential lessons about prayer and the real world. They demonstrate that turning to God in prayer is the simplest and surest way of gaining his protection. The lonely prince surrounded by unspeakable wealth draws comfort only from the Qur'an. Reciting its verses draws him into an unseen family more precious than any hoard of diamonds. And it is the universalism of the Qur'an, recited in the same manner and in the same language throughout the world, which gives Zobeide the courage to approach the prince. Finally, the most powerful lesson of the entire story is conveyed by the soldiers, merchants, courtiers and slaves frozen into stone: solid, petrified reminders that any society, no matter how beautiful its buildings or how rich its treasury, is as lifeless as stone if it turns its back on the call to prayer.

That call to worship which unites fairytale princes and the most down to earth of twentieth-century believers was, it is claimed, first heard by Muhammad, during the *miraj* or Night Ride to Heaven. There, surrounded by the presence of God, Muhammad was told that God, the All-Merciful, who needed nothing, asked for the prayers of the children he had created.

——————————— ∽ ———————————

O ye who believe! When the call is heard for the prayer
of the day of congregation, haste unto remembrance of
Allah and leave your trading. That is better for you if ye
did but know.

Sura 62:9, The Congregation

——————————— ∽ ———————————

That call to prayer and the manner in which it was fulfilled
was the first specifically Islamic practice to develop. To begin
with it was a duty undertaken only by Muhammad but soon,
after he and his followers had fled from persecution in Mecca
to Medina in AD 622 or year 1 of the Muslim calendar, daily
salat became the duty of all Muslims. At first prayers were
said, not facing towards Mecca, but towards Jerusalem. That
quickly changed and from February AD 624 Muslim worshippers were instructed to turn towards Mecca and, more
specifically, towards the Ka'aba, the first house of prayer
dedicated to the 'one unseen but all hearing God'.

For the Muslim prayer is an activity which involves the
body as well as the spirit. The body and the senses are drawn
into the process of prayer – they are neither repressed or
denied. In Muslim society the time for each daily prayer is
announced by the call of the muezzin who tells the faithful
and the unfaithful that God is great, Muhammad is his
Prophet and that the hour for prayer and salvation has come.

At least once a day, prayer must be preceded by ritual
washing. Prayer must always be governed by thirteen *arkan* or
essentials, which dictate exactly what is to be said and done
and the order which these actions and words should follow. It
is the *arkan* which makes *salat* familiar even in a foreign land.

Salat begins with the worshipper standing up and facing
Mecca. All mosques have a mihrab or niche indicating
the correct direction. After a second call to prayer the

worshipper, still standing, recites the opening *Sura* of the Qur'an, a prayer as universal as its God:

───────────────────── ☽ ─────────────────────

In the name of Allah, the Beneficent, the Merciful.
Praise be to Allah, Lord of the Worlds,
The Beneficent, the Merciful.
Owner of the Day of Judgement,
Thee (alone) we worship; Thee (alone) we ask for
 help.
Show us the straight path,
The path of those whom Thou has favoured; Not the
 path of those who earn Thine anger nor of those
 who go astray.

Sura 1, The Opening

───────────────────── ☽ ─────────────────────

This is followed by more recitation of the Qur'an. The worshipper then bows deeply towards Mecca, bending the whole upper part of his body while keeping his hands on his knees. While he bows he recites praise of God. Returning to the standing position he lifts his hands to the side of his face and utters a short prayer. This is followed by a *sujud*, or prostration, in which the worshipper kneels and bends forward so that his hands and forehead touch the ground in a physical expression of the prayer of submission he is saying. He then adopts a half kneeling or half sitting position before making a second *sujud*.

That pattern of praise and action is followed from one to four times depending on the time of day. Each time the cycle of prayer is concluded by the worshipper returning to the half sitting, half kneeling position and reciting the *shahada*, the first pillar of Islam, then pronouncing a blessing on Muhammad, and finally turning his head to either side and saying *salaam* – 'peace be with you'.

Islam is nothing if not practical. The Qur'an itself acknowledges that full observance of *salat* may not always be possible: 'And when ye go forth in the land, it is not sin for you to curtail (your) worship if ye fear that those who disbelieve may attack you. In truth the disbelievers are an open enemy to you.' (*Sura 4:101, Women*)

The process of the fivefold prayer, whether said in isolation or surrounded by fellow believers or in curtailed form in alien lands, draws together the essentials of Islamic belief and practice. Its keynote is praise of God expressed through words and action, accompanied by an acknowledgement of the unity of Islam and the brotherhood of believers which crosses all social and territorial boundaries.

To non-Muslim eyes the precision of the regulations which govern *salat* may seem restrictive, even mechanical, but there is a further dimension to *salat* beyond words and ritual which joins it to the highest levels of Islamic mysticism. In his 'Book of Salvation' Ibn-Sina, the great eleventh-century Persian philosopher-cum-scientist, known in the West as Avicenna, explains that correctly understood prayer is divided into two parts – the outward and the inward – but the two are mutually dependent. The physical movements of *salat* and the prescribed recitations are the discernible evidence of the unseen prayer of the soul. Only those very close to God find unalloyed inward prayer easy and natural; for the vast majority of believers the detailed ritual of *salat* is essential. It is a path to prayer enabling people to set aside time each day when they can forget their own preoccupations and turn towards God.

Salat encompasses all worshippers and all types of prayer – the inward and the outward, the solitary and the shared. Muslims have no equivalent of Christian Sunday services and *salat* is all the sacramental liturgy they need. The main occasion for congregational worship is the midday *salat* each Friday – a practice instituted by Muhammad during his stay in Medina.

This special prayer of the assembly conducted in the mosque conforms to the basic rules of *salat* but in addition it will include a sermon, usually divided into two parts. The *salat* of the Friday noon assembly therefore provides an opportunity for teaching but also it is a visible statement of the unity of Islam.

Salat, the second pillar of Islam, is a comfort and a source of strength for believers. They know that they are not alone and that, in their journey towards God, they have many fellow travellers. Like Zobeide's solitary prince they know that such an assurance is something for which it is worth giving up many treasures.

4

Iram of the Columns
and the Prostitute's Boot

> Believe in Allah and His messenger, and spend of that
> whereof He hath made you trustees; and such of you as
> believe and spend (aright), theirs will be a great reward.
>
> *Sura 57:7, Iron*

The third pillar on the road to God which is Islam is *zakat* or
almsgiving. It is the natural fruit of the first two pillars of
shahada and *salat*. For the Muslim almsgiving is more than an
act of justice or kindness: it is an expression of reverence
before God – an acknowledgement that the world and all its
riches belong to him. All claims of private ownership are sec-
ondary to the simple truth of creation.

The fundamental importance of *zakat* within Islam can be
gauged by two very different stories: the first is as ancient as
any folk tale, and the second, an anecdote which is more than
an anecdote, dates from the Prophet's own lifetime.

The first story concerns a beautiful remote monumental
city called by the Arabs 'Iram of the Columns'. It has coun-
terparts in many cultures. From Stonehenge to Saudi Arabia,
there are tales of cities built by titans and giants. These stories
abound wherever there are megaliths or massive ruins of any
kind which seem beyond mere human engineering.

The builder of Iram of the Columns was a mysterious pre-Islamic warrior hero called Shaddad Ibn Ad, credited by some with having built the Pyramids. Whatever his Egyptian exploits were, there is general agreement that Shaddad Ibn Ad was a fearsome and avaricious conqueror. He and his army conquered every country they entered. They vanquished Armenia, Samarkand and Tibet. They continued their progress as far east as it was possible to go. Returning through Armenia, Shaddad and his men conquered all northern Africa as far west as the Atlantic. Shaddad had much to do and fortunately his lifespan matched his ambitions. He spent a full two hundred years in northern Africa campaigning and building great fortresses before returning to southern Arabia.

There he set about building his fabulous city which he decided would rival Paradise. All the countries he had conquered were scoured for precious materials. The riches of the entire world were lavished on this new city which was, it is said, more majestic than any city which had been built before or has been built since. When Shaddad died after reaching the ripe old age of five hundred all the wealth he had accumulated was buried with him. According to some versions of the story Shaddad and his followers were killed by the divine intervention of a thunderbolt as they rode out to inspect the completed city – like the architects of Babel, they had been too proud and overweening in their achievements.

In the Qur'an, Shaddad's heroic stature is unimportant. All that is mentioned about Iram of the Columns is its doom. For the true believer, wealth is not a private resource to be buried in a tomb or squandered on a godless enterprise, rather it is a blessing from God and should be used as such. In the eyes of the Qur'an Shaddad the hero is unmasked as Shaddad the greedy arrogant fool.

There is a counterbalance to that story. It comes from the Hadith – the collection of traditions recording how the

Prophet and his family and followers put the message of the Qur'an into practice in their daily lives. According to one of these traditions, Muhammad told the story of how one day a prostitute walking past a well noticed a dog lying on its lid. The dog was parched with thirst; its tongue was hanging out but it was unable to reach the water below. Taking pity on the dog, the prostitute took off her boot and her head veil and, tying them together, carefully lowered her boot into the well and drew it out filled with water for the dog. This act of kindness, remarked the Prophet, wiped out the prostitute's sin. For the Muslim believer anyone, no matter how lowly, can give. In the end the prostitute with the wet boot was richer than Shaddad the hoarder of Iram of the Columns because she, by giving, had received the wealth of forgiveness.

For the Muslim almsgiving is a simple and natural extension of faith and prayer. It is an act which is described as a means of purifying the soul. It can atone for sin – particularly sins of selfishness and extravagance. The Qur'an makes it clear that giving to one's own family, to those without family, to travellers, to beggars or to anyone in need, is part of the piety. But the mere act of giving is not enough. The Qur'an insists that the motive behind any almsgiving is of paramount importance: almsgiving merely for the sake of ostentation counts for little. True giving is undertaken for the sake of fulfilling God's will; while it is perfectly acceptable to let people know of your generosity, it is even better to give secretly.

Zakat is usually taken to refer to the obligatory charity tax levied in some Muslim communities but that is not the limit to almsgiving. It also includes *sadaqa* – acts of charity beyond that which is legally prescribed. Islamic law lays down detailed regulations about the ways of calculating *zakat* on livestock, precious metals and various other possessions, but in many places this has been simplified to a straighforward yearly 2½ per cent levy on a family's bank balance – less extreme than the Judaeo-Christian tithe but more observed in practice.

——————————— ᠕ ———————————

> It is not righteousness that ye turn your faces to the East and the West; but righteous is he who believeth in Allah and the Last Day and the angels and the Scripture and the prophets; and giveth wealth, for love of Him, to kinsfolk and to orphans and the needy and the wayfarer and to those who ask, and to set slaves free; and observeth proper worship and payeth the poor-due. And those who keep their treaty when they make one, and the patient in tribulation and adversity and time of stress. Such are they who are sincere. Such are the God-fearing.
>
> *Sura 2:177, The Cow*

——————————— ᠕ ———————————

Almsgiving is for all – not just the rich. But Muhammad tried to ensure that his followers kept a sense of proportion about giving. He reminded them that they were not called on to beggar themselves but to give freely of their surplus. Those who have no surplus can still observe the third pillar of Islam by *acting* charitably. Protecting people from harm, helping them cheerfully, settling quarrels and each step taken to prayer is charity.

The practice of almsgiving is deeply rooted in the Muslim community. Even before Muhammad's flight from Mecca to Medina, the fledgling Islamic family set great store by helping the poor, regardless of faith. After the flight to Medina, when the refugees from the Meccan persecution suddenly found themselves dependent on the Muslims of Medina, the value of almsgiving as an internal welfare system soon became obvious. *Zakat* became the means of putting the theory of the brotherhood of Islam into practice.

From its earliest days Islam has been a political as well as a theological movement. Muhammad was not only a religious teacher but also a social reformer and a radical lawgiver. Islam points to an ideal society where all believers are equal and ancient tribal loyalties and privilege are submerged into a more universal vision of brotherhood. Muhammad put that vision into practice in his own life. When he fled to Medina, he renounced the ancient 'laws of blood'. This meant that he rejected the rights and protection due to him because of his ties of kinship. In a sense he had made himself an outlaw, but in doing so, he freed himself to teach the truth of the brother-hood of all believers. Antecedents no longer mattered – faith did. The laws of clanship round Mecca and Medina went into decline and the law of the larger family of faith quickly took its place.

─────────────── ୰ ───────────────

So give to the kinsman his due, and to the needy, and to the wayfarer. That is best for those who seek Allah's Countenance. And such are they who are successful.

That which ye give in usury in order that it may increase on (other) people's property hath no increase with Allah; but that which ye give in charity, seeking Allah's Countenance, hath increase manifold.

Sura 30:38 & 39, The Romans

─────────────── ୰ ───────────────

Those in need in the community were bolstered by *zakat*, but there was yet another sort of generosity which Muham-mad taught. He tried to mould a society where fairness replaced usury in financial affairs. He condemned those who clung on to ancient privileges such as inherited wealth – an individual should not be judged by the wealth of his family but the strength of his faith. 'What is pride in ancestry?' he asked, 'but a staked claim in property.' It proved nothing about a person's worth whereas generosity was evidence of true piety. Muhammad also ensured that women were touched by this new spirit of fairness. He introduced more equitable divorce law, limited the extent of polygamy and ensured women had the right to inherit. Husbands, he reminded his followers, do not own their wives, rather they have them on trust from God and should treat them accordingly.

Muhammad tried to instil into his people a sense of justice, commonsense and humility before God. He taught that almsgiving benefited both those who gave and those who received. In fact, both are essential for the health of society. In Islam there is no need for the recipient to feel guilty or beholden to his benefactor. His action of acceptance is as necessary as the act of generosity – it is all part of the process of charity.

Such an idea needed a certain amount of explaining, particularly to the hard-headed merchants and businessmen of Mecca. To get the idea over, Muhammad told a parable as others had done before him. A passenger ship, he said, was plying its trade at sea. Some passengers had places on the upper deck and some had places on the lower deck. There was plenty of water for everyone but it was only available via the upper deck. This meant that passengers from below deck had to come to the upper deck whenever they were thirsty. Some of the lower deck passengers had an idea. They thought that if they bored holes through the sides of the ship they could have enough water without having to trouble those above. The fate of all those on the ship depended on the ability of those on the upper deck to persuade those below not to cause everyone's death by drowning but to let go their pride and, for the good of all, to continue accepting the water from above.

Almsgiving, then, is a two-way process benefiting all those involved. At one level, it is a simple exercise in commonsense, but for the Muslim there is a deeper level as well. All the pillars of Islam share a common motive – the desire to please God. This underlying purpose lifts acts of practical charity to the level of mysticism. The giver increases the richness of his faith by practising detachment from material things and, by his action, proclaims the message that is Islam.

Muslims do not share Christians' guilt about wealth. They do not have to worry about camels and the eyes of needles. *Zakat*, dutifully observed, saves them from the burden of riches. It is a tax to be taken seriously. The Hadith contains dire warnings about the punishments awaiting those who fail to pay their due. *Zakat* can cleanse, but if ignored it can also condemn.

To the non-Muslim it may seem over zealous to equate failure to do good with sin but it must be remembered that *zakat* points to a truth larger than any single act of giving. Everything belongs to God, regardless of who is temporarily acting as its steward, and therefore everything should be disposed of according to his will.

There is a story told of a rich merchant who every winter equipped his household with braziers, rich rugs and heavy clothes. When spring came he would give everything away to the poor and would buy feathered fans and cool clothes for the summer instead. At the end of summer he would once again give everything away. His financial advisers tried to dissuade him from continuing to run his affairs this way. They pointed out it made no economic sense to give away goods which you could be certain would have to be replaced in six months' time. The merchant was not to be swayed. If God had allowed him to enjoy riches through a summer or a winter, he was right to share with others the benefit he had received. But what if his fortunes failed, he was asked. Then, he said, no one could take away the enjoyment he had received and ultimately the fortunes were not his but God's so he would not even be a loser.

Islam is neither communism nor capitalism. Wealth offers opportunity, but it entails responsibility too. There is no sanction for efficient greed. When the city of Medina was struck by famine, Othman, the third of the rightly-guided caliphs, could have sold off food at ten times its usual price; instead he gave it away – that was his duty.

In an Islamic society those in positions of authority are the guardians of almsgiving. If *zakat* does not meet the needs of the people it is up to those in power to ensure the poor do not suffer – if necessary by levying additional alms taxes.

Zakat should not be seen as evidence for the legalism of Islam. It is faith in action which at times may seem to run counter to economic self-interest. Above all it is a means of praising God. Almsgiving elevates the prostitute with her wet boot above Shaddad, the legendary warrior king, who thought he was rich but did not know his own poverty. *Zakat* is an invitation to share in the work of God and acquire a sense of proportion so that, with the Prophet, the true believer can say 'God gives: I am only a distributor.'

5

A Broken Jug and a Stew
of Fishes' Tongues

The month of Ramadan in which was revealed the
Qur'an, a guidance for mankind, and clear proofs of the
guidance, and the Criterion (of right and wrong). And
whosoever of you is present, let him fast the month, and
whosoever of you is sick or on a journey, (let him fast
the same) number of other days.

Sura 2:185, The Cow

Fasting has a place in many religious traditions. It is a link
which binds the Abrahamic family of faith to the wider world
of belief, ancient and modern. The ancient Egyptians fasted
before going to the temple. Most of the great mystery religions associated with mother goddesses like Cybele and
Demeter required their devotees to fast before taking part in
their secret rituals. Down the centuries there has been a conviction that elective fasting sharpens the perceptions and
opens the mind to non-worldly dimensions of being.

For the Muslim, *sawm* or fasting (in Urdu *roza*) is the fourth
pillar of Islam. It is at one and the same time a penance and a
celebration of free will. During the great thirty-day fast of
Ramadan, Muslims eat and drink nothing between sunrise
and sunset. To non-Muslims this may seem a daunting endur-

ance test, particularly in countries with hot climates. There may seem at first glance to be no immediately obvious religious benefit, but set in the context of belief *sawm* represents more than a month's ritual fasting. It is an expression both of moderation in human desires and submission to the will of God.

As with all the pillars of Islam, *sawm* should be observed by all believers regardless of personal circumstances or temperament. For the Sufis, the followers of the mystic tradition within Islam, *sawm* was and is part of their ascetic way of life, but for all Muslims the practice of fasting engenders a sense of proportion and balance into their lives. This is true for both rich and poor, worldly and unworldly, as two stories about two very different believers demonstrate.

The first concerns the poet mystic Rabia who lived in the eighth century. Her life was one of extreme material poverty. At first this was not a matter of choice. She was born into a family living at subsistence level. Orphaned at an early age, she was kidnapped and sold into slavery. One night her owner heard her praying and to his amazement noticed a lamp hanging above her head although there was nothing attaching it to the ceiling. Frightened, he decided the best course of action would be to free this strange slave. Rabia leapt at the chance of freedom and made her way to the desert where she chose a life of poverty more severe than anything she had previously been forced to endure. Her one purpose in life became seeking and fulfilling the will of God.

One night, after she had been fasting night and day for an entire week, Rabia stopped praying and was suddenly overwhelmed by hunger. At that moment a friend came to her home and gave her a bowl of food. Delighted at the opportune gift, Rabia went to fetch a lamp to eat by. When she returned she found the bowl was empty. It had been knocked over by a cat. Rabia made up her mind that she would still break her fast even if it meant only slaking her thirst with water. So she went out to fetch some water and as she returned indoors with a full jug, the lamp gutted. In the darkness the jug of water slipped out of her hands and smashed on the floor, so she was left with neither food nor water.

In sheer frustration she called on God asking him why he was letting such misfortune fall on her. A voice came to her warning her that she could not want her own material comfort and the will of God equally. She would have to work out priorities. Rabia accepted that lesson and from that moment on ensured that no wish was ever stronger than her desire for God.

Rabia is revered as a saint and a teacher. She was a woman of exceptional holiness, but the incident of the broken jug shows that even those who own very little and are very close to God can deepen their faith by fasting. No one is too poor or too holy to be able to benefit from putting the desire for God before their own instinctive wants.

But the rich and worldly learn too from the sense of moderation taught by *sawm*. Harun al-Rashid, the Caliph of Baghdad, lived at roughly the same time as Rabia but there all similarity apparently ended. His was a life of luxury, sophistication and power. He is said to have corresponded with the Emperor Charlemagne and to have sent him a water clock and a pet baby elephant as gifts. He was a confident survivor in a world of international politics and also in the more deadly world of palace intrigue. Baghdad during his reign was a place of fabulous wealth: the houses of the rich were full of silk and porcelain from China, ivory and spices from Africa and precious jewels from India.

However, wealth does not have to be synonymous with selfishness. The story is told of how one day Harun was being entertained to dinner by his brother. A delicate fish stew was put before the caliph. Intrigued by the unusual dish Harun asked why all the pieces of fish were so minute. His brother proudly explained it was because the dish was entirely composed of fishes' tongues. Harun refused to be party to such extravagance which he said was unworthy of a believer. He enquired the price of the dish and insisted that an equivalent sum immediately be given to the poor. He even ordered that the ornate dish the stew had been presented on should be given away.

Harun was no paragon of asceticism but he followed the path of the pillars of Islam. Like Rabia, he drew lessons from his faith which enabled him to inject a sense of proportion in his life. The part played by *sawm* in the life of each believer, whether saint or sinner, introduces an element of balance and questioning. Appetites, whether for a hermit's supper or a caliph's feast, need to be scrutinised and submitted to the will of God.

Islam is not a discipline for fanatics. Fasting is only part of the believer's life. The Hadith record that Muhammad's wife Aisha warned against the sort of uncontrolled fasting which destroyed God-given health. *Sawm* must never become an end in itself. It is only useful if it is used as a means of bringing each Muslim's life closer to God. It is an exercise in self-discipline and free will which, according to the Qur'an, shows the difference between men and women who strive to follow God and the beasts of the field who only have to satisfy themselves.

Sawm has been part of the Muslim way of life from the earliest days. One year after the flight from Mecca to Medina, in year 2 of the Muslim calendar, Muhammad called for an annual twenty-four-hour fast. The fast was referred to as the *ashura* or tenth. The word *ashura* points to a link between Jewish and Muslim practices since it was the word used by the Jews of southern Arabia for their fast on the Day of Atonement. The fast of Ramadan evolved quickly the following year after Muhammad's great battle of Badr in the month of Ramadan when he led three hundred of his followers against one thousand Meccans and overcame the unpromising odds to inflict a decisive defeat on the Meccan army.

The month of Ramadan then became doubly sacred to Muhammad and his followers. Not only did it mark their first major armed victory but it was already the month of the Night of Destiny: it was on the twenty-seventh night of Ramadan that the first words of the Qur'an were revealed to the Prophet on Mount Hira. The fast of Ramadan and recitation of the Qur'an are intertwined. Believers are encouraged to recite one-thirtieth of the Qur'an each night of the fast – food for the spirit during the month of hunger.

The mood of Ramadan is one of reflection. The fast not only affects the individual but also the whole community. Inevitably, in a predominantly Muslim area, the pace of life slows down. Ramadan is a time for taking stock and mending old quarrels.

———————— ☽ ————————

The month of Ramadan in which was revealed the Qur'an, a guidance for mankind, and clear proofs of the guidance, and the Criterion (of right and wrong). And whosoever of you is present, let him fast the month, and whosoever of you is sick or on a journey, (let him fast the same) number of other days. Allah desireth for you ease; He desireth not hardship for you; and (He desireth) that ye should complete the period, and that ye should magnify Allah for having guided you, and that peradventure ye may be thankful.

Sura 2:185, The Cow

———————— ☽ ————————

The regulations of the fast are set out clearly in the Qur'an. The requirements are challenging, but not inhuman. Those who are unwell, or who need to eat and drink to complete a journey in health, are allowed to make up the days of broken fast as soon as it is reasonable to do so. Women who need to keep their strength up because they are losing blood either through menstruation or childbirth are also absolved from the need to fast. Everyone is allowed to eat and drink in the hours of darkness – until, the Qur'an states, it becomes possible to distinguish a white thread from a black one by natural light.

The daylight fast does not apply only to food and drink. Believers are also required to abstain from sex. Many regard smoking too as against the spirit of the fast. During Ramadan there is also the expectation that Muslims should control what they say. Words which might cause hurt, anger or indecent thoughts are incompatible with Ramadan too.

Muhammad described *sawm* as a form of worship, the one, he said, which was loved most by God since only He knew whether it had been faithfully observed and at what cost to each believer, and only He would reward it.

The Qur'an is realistic as well as idealistic. It says that not everyone will succeed in meeting the demands of fasting. In such cases where willpower is weak, those unable to fulfil the requirements of *sawm* can at least make sure that they feed the hungry. This is a poor second-best but it is better than nothing.

According to one of the traditions told about the Prophet, he described a completed fast as a cause for double celebration. First, the faithful believer has the simple joy of achievement; secondly, believers who have fulfilled the duty of *sawm* will know that, when they meet God, their breath will not smell of the staleness of fasting – to God it will smell sweeter than musk perfume.

Sawm is not an act of solitary self-improvement. The three-day feast of Id al-Fitr which marks the end of Ramadan is also the time for giving. The month as a whole is not a period of gloom: it is for self-discipline but also for communal celebration. As night falls on each day of Ramadan, Muslims hold *Iftar* – literally 'break-fast' – parties for their families and friends.

Ramadan – the month of fasting and remembering the providence of God – is an annual event in the Muslim calendar. It seems to move restlessly across the solar Gregorian calendar but that is because the Muslim calendar has only twelve lunar months. This means that each year every feast and festival moves thirteen days earlier. So Ramadan moves slowly through the season, preceded each year by Laila Al-Bar'h, the Night of Forgiveness, when believers in preparation for the fast seek to heal old wounds and apologise for wrongs committed so that their fasting may be untainted by any selfishness or injustice perpetrated over the previous twelve months.

For the believer *sawm* means much more than depriving oneself of food and drink: properly performed it is a fast of the soul as well as the body. It is completely against the purposes of Ramadan to observe the forms of the fast but to lie and cheat. According to tradition, Muhammad said there was no point in someone spreading falsehood and keeping up the fast – God would have no need of such a believer's fast.

Sawm undertaken by hypocrites is meaningless, but attempted wholeheartedly, the Prophet told Mu'adh bin Jabal as recorded in the Hadith, it is a sure protection against the fires of hell. The pillar of fasting is also the pillar of freedom. Its observance helps believers to appreciate that they are in control of their appetites. It gives them a sense of their ability to respond to the will of God and a sense of proportion which is not governed by selfishness. *Sawm* is also the pillar of thanksgiving and pride in the capacity of men and women to be more than the slaves of either hunger or luxury. It is a practice which can form the lives of all believers whether the saintliest of ascetics or the worldliest of rulers and bring them closer to God.

6

In the Footsteps of
Adam and Abraham

Lo! The first Sanctuary appointed for mankind was that at Mecca, a blessed place, a guidance to the peoples;

Wherein are plain memorials (of Allah's guidance); the place where Abraham stood up to pray; and whosoever entereth it is safe. And pilgrimage to the House is a duty unto Allah for mankind, for him who can find a way thither.

Sura 3:96 & 97, The Family of Imran

Every year, in the month of Dhuil-Hijja, hundreds of thousands of Muslims converge on the holy city of Mecca in Saudi Arabia. They come from every walk of life and every continent. They are united only by their faith in the one God and in his Prophet Muhammad and by their determination to complete the *hajj* – the arduous pilgrimage which is the fifth pillar of Islam.

Muslims have been making their way to Mecca ever since the lifetime of the Prophet. Now the *hajj* is performed by a greater number of pilgrims than ever before. But although between 1½ and 2 million believers complete the pilgrimage each year, this still means that, for the vast majority of Muslims, *hajj* is an unattainable dream.

For Christians reared on the Canterbury Tales and familiar with innumerable brochures offering package holidays to
pilgrim sites, the intensity of the demands of *hajj* is far
removed from their own experience. *Hajj* is not a jolly holy
holiday. It is a rigorous process of purification, every level
laden with symbolism, which expresses the unity of believers
and their complete submission to the will of God. Every pilgrim, whether entrepreneur or factory worker, professor or
peasant, surrenders autonomy over his or her life and obeys
the rules of *hajj* which are blind to social, racial or cultural
distinctions.

And it has always been so. Mughal court records describe
how in the sixteenth century Gulbadan, the daughter of the
great Babur, the first Mughal emperor of India, the sister of
Humayan, the second emperor, and the aunt of Akbar, the
third emperor, decided to make the pilgrim journey to
Mecca. Akbar financed the journey, provided an entourage
and even accompanied his aunt on the first stage of her route
from Agra to Ajoner, walking humbly, dressed in the seam-
less white robe of a pilgrim. But even an emperor could not
completely smooth the pilgrim way. Gulbadan's journey was
to take years. There were difficulties over travel documents
causing a delay of twelve months. Part of the problem was
securing papers insisted on by the Portuguese who controlled
the sea routes from western India to Arabia. Not realising
that Muslims revered Jesus and Mary, the Portuguese
ordered that every pilgrim had to have a pass stamped with a
seal depicting the two. Of course the intended insult fell wide
of its mark.

The sea voyage over, the harshness of the overland journey
began, mitigated to some extent by Akbar's provisions. Once
the holy city was entered Gulbadan's life was transformed.
She and her court ladies exchanged their fine clothes for the
simple robes of pilgrims. Accustomed to avoiding the sun and

the heat, they had to undertake the strenuous sevenfold race between the hill of Safa and the Mount Marwa and then the journey to Mount Arafat where Muhammad preached his final sermon. Finally they and their fellow pilgrims returned to Mecca to join the press of believers circling the Ka'aba, the holy shrine.

Gulbadan delighted in her new life. She remained in Arabia for nearly four years making the *hajj* four times. In the end Akbar sent a ship to bring her home. The homeward journey was fraught with difficulty and delay: the ship was wrecked and the returning pilgrims were stranded in Aden. Eventually, after more than six years' absence, Gulbadan returned to Agra. The Emperor himself met them on the final leg of their journey and bombarded them with questions. As a mark of respect, Gulbadan and her ladies were given control of the imperial seal – even a princess achieved greater status by the accomplishment of the *hajj*.

The journey to Mecca today takes less time, but for the majority of pilgrims it is still an exercise in endurance as well as faith. Over the years, the Meccan pilgrim ships have been a byword for discomfort, overcrowding and straightforward danger. Travel conditions have improved to some extent, but they are still far from easy. The completion of *hajj* is still a feat to be proud of. In any Nubian village on the banks of the Nile you will find the walls of houses proudly painted with pictures of trucks, trains and aeroplanes, indicating that inside there is a returned pilgrim and recording his or her means of arriving at the holy city.

Recent years have brought new difficulties. There are now so many pilgrims that the ritual sacrifice of a sheep or goat or camel would result in an embarrassing sacrificed meat mountain. In theory the meat should be given to the poor but the pilgrims' sacrifices are now far in excess of the appetites of Mecca's poor. Fears that extremists will use the *hajj* to launch publicity-seeking terrorism have brought a tangle of new security measures, and, while acts of terrorism have increased the dangers, the growing numbers of pilgrims have strained the resources of Mecca. However, Gulbadan would notice some improvements. The sevenfold race between Marwa and Safa is no longer at the mercy of the elements – the Saudi Arabian government has built an air-conditioned, marble-floored corridor.

But not all the twentieth-century improvements are welcomed. There are complaints about the newly-completed flyovers and multi-lane motorways which contribute unwanted noise and pollution. Western-style hotels have also drawn criticism. The point of *hajj* is that all believers are equal before God therefore all material difference should become irrelevant. When the pilgrim cry *labbaika* goes up it should be from a brotherhood of believers bound by faith, not divided by social advantage and disadvantage.

The *hajj* will survive the excesses of the twentieth century. Unlike many other places of pilgrimage it is not connected with one holy life or a single incident. The pilgrimage to the Ka'aba is built on many layers of tradition stretching back through the stories of Abraham, Hagar and Ishmael, and to the wanderings of Adam, the first man and the first prophet. And many Muslims believe that the origins of the Ka'aba, the first temple to the one God, lie outside created time and outside the small world of men.

According to one of the Hadiths, when Ali, the great grandson of Muhammad, was in Mecca completing the *hajj*, he was approached by a man from Jerusalem, a god-seeker who had read both the Torah of the Jews and the Gospel of the Christians and wanted to know why Muslims went on *hajj* and why it took the form of circling the Ka'aba. When he had finished praying Ali began to teach the questioner from Jerusalem. He told him that the beginnings of the Ka'aba predated the creation of man. When God told his angels that he intended to give the earth to man as his kingdom, the angels were amazed. Why, they asked, give such power and privilege to a creature who would fall into sin and allow the earth to become a place of bloodshed and corruption? Would it not be better, they suggested, to put the earth under angelic control and then its future would be secure – it would be a place of obedience and praise. God listened to his angels and gently reminded them that he knew more than they did.

Suddenly the angels realised they had come near to contradicting the will of God. They immediately backed down and approached the throne of God with great humility. As a sign of their repentance they circled the throne for three hours and God gazed at them with compassion and love. And God decreed that beneath his heavenly throne a special building should be constructed on four emerald columns inlaid with rubies. This, God said, would become the angels' new house of praise. So the angels withdrew from the throne of God and instead circled their new temple. God was pleased, and instructed them to see to it that a similar house was built on earth so that mortal men and women could praise God on earth just as the angels praise him in heaven.

That was the extent of Ali's lesson. When he had finished, the questioner, perhaps an angel in disguise, told Ali that he had answered well and spoken nothing but the truth.

Other traditions continue the story and explain why the heavenly house of praise came to be copied at Mecca. It is said that after Adam was expelled from Paradise God told him he must build a house of praise like the one he had been shown in heaven and he and his descendants must circle it as he had seen the angels do in heaven. Adam wandered through Arabia looking for the centre point of the earth. Finally he came to a low hill set in a valley surrounded by mountains. On the hill was a luminous white stone, a heavenly symbol of man's soul. This he knew was where he must begin building what would become the Ka'aba. He set to work recreating the heavenly house of ruby and emerald with stone, some collected from Mount Sinai, some from the Mount of Olives, some from Mount Lebanon and some from the mountain where one day the ark of the prophet Noah would rest. Adam completed his work and worshipped his creator there.

Many, many years passed. The sands of time obliterated every trace of Adam's temple and eventually the waters of the Great Flood covered the earth. Noah afloat in his ark sailed over the land which had been and would once again be the desert of Arabia. When the ark passed over the spot where Adam had fulfilled God's command, it circled the sunken Ka'aba seven times.

Long after the flood had disappeared and God had promised Noah that the earth would never be destroyed by water again, the Prophet and Patriarch Abraham came to the valley of the hidden temple. He was accompanied by Hagar, his maidservant, and Ishmael, the son she had borne him. Just by the low hill which now covered Adam's Ka'aba, Abraham abandoned Hagar and Ishmael to the will of God. Soon Hagar's few pitiful provisions of a handful of dates and a skin of water were exhausted. Frantically she called on God's help. Leaving her child in the shade of the low hill she ran to the hill of Safa but could see no trace of water. She ran to Mount Marwa but again found nothing. Seven times she made the journey, desperately checking and double-checking.

Hearing a voice, she returned to the low hill where she had left her son. There she saw an angel who asked her why she was weeping. She replied simply 'I thirst', just as every pilgrim who has retraced her steps thirsts for God. The angel touched the earth of the low hill with his wing and immediately a spring of pure water bubbled out of the ground.

That water still flows today and has been drunk by pilgrims down the centuries. It is known as the spring of Zamzam, the name recreating the sound of its rushing waters.

Hagar and Ishmael thrived. They settled by the spring and were given sheep and goats in return for allowing nomadic herdsmen to water their flocks at the spring. In due course Hagar died, Abraham returned and was reunited with his son. Together they began their greatest work. Over the exact site of Adam's Ka'aba, they began to build a temple to the one God, and Abraham placed the sacred stone, once white but now blackened by men's sins, inside the sanctuary.

The new Ka'aba was not an elaborate building – just a simple rectangular enclosure – but its purpose lifted it above the intricacies of pagan temples. Before Abraham left Ishmael and the house of prayer, he prayed to God and asked for a messenger or a prophet to come and guide his son's people. Ishmael and his descendants tended the Ka'aba until the war-like Amalekites surrounded it. Ishmael's family yielded the Ka'aba rather than see it polluted by bloodshed. The Ka'aba was to endure many more trials: it would be destroyed by harsh weather and rebuilt, squabbled and fought over. Worst of all, its original purpose would be subverted: it would become a temple of idol worship and polytheism. Only with the coming of Muhammad and his cleansing of the Ka'aba in AD 630 would the earthly house of praise resume its sacred task of reflecting the praise of heaven.

By instituting the *hajj*, Muhammad was not advocating some new religious practice. He was trying to bind Muslims of the present and the future to their earliest ancestors in faith. As Muslims begin their journey to Mecca, they are resuming the search of Adam. Many of them echo the ancient formula 'In the name of God be the course and the mooring', the prayer of Noah as he began his voyage in the ark. All of them recreate Hagar's frantic search for water. On top of this pilgrims bring the prayers and concerns of their own lives. They hope by the *hajj* to cleanse themselves of present sin and to ensure in the future a more faithful and wholehearted submission to God. They also have the promise made by God to Abraham that all believers who come to venerate the holy house will find that their relationship with their Lord is strengthened.

Hajj contains within it many elements. As well as commemorating the prophets, the past, and Muhammad's triumph over polytheism, it is an opportunity for each Muslim to look ahead to his or her own future. As the faithful gather dressed in the simple white robes of pilgrimage, they anticipate the Day of Judgement which awaits all believers. The Ka'aba, the centre of their attention, becomes the link which binds them to a past and a future beyond their own lifetimes.

———————————————— ∪ ————————————————

Perform the pilgrimage and the visit (to Mecca) for Allah. And if ye are prevented, then send such gifts as can be obtained with ease, and shave not your heads until the gifts have reached their destination. And whoever among you is sick or hath an ailment of the head must pay a ransom of fasting or almsgiving or offering. And if ye are in safety, then whosoever contenteth himself with the visit for the pilgrimage (shall give) such gifts as can be had with ease. And whosoever cannot find (such gifts), then a fast of three days while on the pilgrimage, and of seven when ye have returned; that is, ten in all. This is for him whose folk are not present at the Inviolable Place of Worship. Observe your duty to Allah, and know that Allah is severe in punishment.

The pilgrimage is (in) the well-known months, and whoever is minded to perform the pilgrimage therein (let him remember that) there is (to be) no lewdness nor abuse nor angry conversation on the pilgrimage. And

whatsoever good ye do Allah knoweth it. So make provision for yourselves (hereafter); for the best provision
is to ward off evil. Therefore keep your duty unto Me,
O men of understanding.

Sura 2:196 & 197, The Cow

───────────────────── ৬ ─────────────────────

The experience of *hajj* is no light undertaking and it is
greater than the personal devotion of each believer. It is a
statement of the brotherhood of faith. This is why *hajj* cannot
be undertaken at the whim or the convenience of pilgrims but
must be started in a specific month. A shorter, less demanding
version of the *hajj* – known as the lesser *hajj* or visitation to
Mecca – can, it is true, be taken at any time of year, but if
believers are strong enough they are encouraged to take the
lesser *hajj* straight after the main *hajj* – thus remaining in the
state of ritual purity. But Islam is nothing if not practical: if
pilgrims find the prospect of the *hajj* followed by the lesser
hajj too much, they are allowed to begin with the lesser *hajj*
and then recuperate for a few days before once again putting
on pilgrim garb and setting out on the greater *hajj*.

Hajj is only open to participants – it is not a spectacle for
onlookers. The pilgrims who crowd into Mecca enter the
haram – that is a sanctuary where no non-believer may enter.
Some non-Muslims have claimed that they have penetrated
the sacred cordon of faith but their accounts are treated with
some scepticism by believers, although the claims of the Vic-
torian explorer Sir Richard Francis Burton have been
accepted. Modern would-be Burtons have to face far more
sophisticated security measures as well as the prospect of
sparking off an outcry of international indignation.

The complexities of *hajj* are daunting enough for believers.
In the first week of the month of pilgrimage newcomers to
Mecca are helped by a corps of guides through the order of
prayer, circling the Ka'aba, drinking from the spring

Zamzam and following in Hagar's footsteps. The opening ceremonies take place on the seventh day of the month of pilgrimage when the Ka'aba itself is purified and the introductory sermon is preached. On the next day all the pilgrims make their way to the small deserted village of Mina some five miles east of Mecca, where they gather and spend the night. For those taking part, this vast sea of white robed figures is an unforgettable image of the unity and transcendence of Islam. Even the simple act of assembly is for most an intensely moving experience – a vision of the future perhaps when the dead will be raised.

On the following day, day nine, the huge crowd makes its way to the Plain of Arafat which lies a further ten miles to the east. Many pilgrims set out earlier for Arafat because the huge numbers now attracted by the *hajj* have slowed the pace down. The time of departure is not as important as the time of arrival: every pilgrim wants to be at Arafat in time to say midday prayers there.

There is a small hillock on the Plain of Arafat called the Mount of Mercy. There pilgrims stand until sunset performing the *wuquf*, literally 'standing', ceremony and listening to a sermon commemorating the one preached by Muhammad on his farewell pilgrimage. The ritual ends at sunset when, at the sound of cannonfire, the entire pilgrim body begins to run towards the Valley of Muzdalifa which lies about halfway back to the assembly point at Mina.

In the valley pilgrims recite evening prayers and have some refreshment. They scour the ground for pebbles which they will use later for the ceremony of 'stoning the devil'. Ideally, each pilgrim should equip themselves with forty-nine stones not smaller than a chicken's egg. Male pilgrims spend the night at Muzdalifa, while women, children and the less fit men return to the camp at Mina for the night.

The following day, all the pilgrims converge on Mina.

Over the next three days they turn their attention to a stone pillar known as Jamrat al-Aqaba which symbolises the devil: each pilgrim denounces Satan as he or she throws the recently collected pebbles at it. Once again the popularity of the *hajj* has brought problems – it is hard to get near enough for a good shot and quite a few pilgrims succeed only in stoning fellow pilgrims. However, it is intention rather than marksmanship which counts.

All that remains for the pilgrims to do is *Id al-Adha* – the feast of sacrifice – with the offering of a sheep, goat or camel at Mina followed by a celebratory meal. The pilgrims know that they are joined, not only by the vast press of people they can see, but by Muslims all over the world; they are also celebrating with the Prophet Abraham who, although willing to sacrifice his son in obedience to God's will, joyfully sacrificed a ram instead. *Id al-Adha* thus combines a celebration of the obedience of the faithful with a celebration of the mercy of God.

When the meal of *Id al-Adha* is over, the pilgrims shave their heads or cut a lock of their hair. Having washed and put on fresh clothes, they return to Mecca to circle the Ka'aba and complete their *hajj*. As each pilgrim performs his or her final circling of the Ka'aba they know that they are treading in the footsteps of angels and prophets, of princesses and paupers, and of past believers and believers yet to be born, but above all they know they have submitted to the wishes of God and have fulfilled the fifth pillar of Islam.

7

The Holy Struggle

Fight in the way of Allah against those who fight against you, but begin not hostilities. Lo! Allah loveth not aggressors.

And slay them wherever ye find them, and drive them out of the places whence they drove you out, for persecution is worse than slaughter. And fight not with them at the Inviolable Place of Worship until they first attack you there, but if they attack you (there) then slay them. Such is the reward of disbelievers.

But if they desist, then lo! Allah is Forgiving, Merciful.

And fight them until persecution is no more, and religion is for Allah. But if they desist, then let there be no hostility except against wrong-doers.

Sura 2:190–193, The Cow

For many years, until very recent times, the menacing thud of a mortar fired from a cannon has broken through the calm of one particular summer evening in Ankara, the capital of Turkey. Ankara is a modern city, Muslim by temperament but not formally bound by the strictures of the *Sharia*, the law of Islam. The cannonfire was not the opening salvo of a fanatical protest against the ways of the twentieth century which allows alcohol to be drunk, women to walk with heads uncovered and recidivist thieves to keep both their hands. The mortar was fired as the sign that another Muslim campaign, but not a military one, has successfully been completed. It was the signal that the lunar month of Ramadan was over. Once again Muslims would be able to eat, drink and have sex in the hours of daylight without infringing the fast of Ramadan, one of the five pillars of Islam revealed to Muhammad, the visionary of Mecca, as the perfected path of submission to the God of Adam and Abraham, the God of Moses and Jesus, the one God worshipped by a fifth of the world's population as Allah, the All Merciful, the Lord of Compassion.

It is a fact of world politics that Islam is perceived not as a creed of peace-making compassion, but as an excuse for antique savagery and manic extremism. Muslims have to face the implications of the truth that for many non-Muslims the very word Islam conjures up images of contemporary horror – young men beating their heads until the skin breaks and looking forward to martyrdom, or the anguished faces of hostages caught in the deadly mesh of Lebanese politics.

These images have more to do with the odd amalgam of fear and envy which have for so long characterised relations between the West and the Arab world than with the theology of Islam. In the past, the Arab world gave the West onions, violins, apricots, rosary beads and zero, but these gifts have long been taken for granted. More recently the West has been fascinated by news footage of black-robed women swarming through the streets of Tehran, by death sentences called for or carried out, and by gossip-page accounts of the antics of the petro-dollar rich for whom ridiculous wealth is pocket money. In a world which seeks reassurance in bogeymen, the yellow peril has turned pink, the reds under the bed have gone mauve with *glasnost*, but at least the extremists of the Muslim world remain reliably mad, bad and dangerous to know.

It is time for some facts. Only rampaging Muslims are on the rampage – the vast majority of them are not. It is as foolish to judge Islam by its excesses as it is dishonest to portray the West only by its successes. Islam is not hell-bent on world domination. Far from winning the statistics game, Muslims will be the first to admit that they have not even begun to study the rules. There are no accurate figures for adherence to the Islamic faith, nor is there any masterplan for world conversion.

But this lack of organisation brings with it larger problems. How can mainline Islam avoid being kidnapped by its extremists – or is it already too late? Are the ancient words of the Qur'an and its battery of strictures really persuasive enough to distract young Muslim men and women from the lure of the twentieth century? Is there a genuinely viable middle path between compromise and fanaticism? Or is Islam on a collision course with the modern world?

From the earliest days there have been tensions within Islam which have sought solution on the battlefield and Muslims have never been slow to fight for faith. So much so that the *jihad* – often translated as holy war – has been seen as the unofficial sixth pillar of Islam. It is an aggressive term which seems to confirm all the worst prejudices about Islam – but only, according to Jabal Buaben, a Muslim from Ghana, because it has been half understood.

Jihad, he says, is a very sensitive technical term in Islam. It consists of two branches – the lesser *jihad* and the greater *jihad*. The greater *jihad* is the *jihad* of one's own self, the *jihad* of the soul. The Qur'an says that man was created primarily for the worship of God. People therefore must strive to achieve this. Striving or struggle, in Arabic, is *jihad*. Struggling to worship God – to live a monotheistic life according to the moral principles in the Scriptures – is in itself a greater *jihad*. The lesser *jihad*, which involves use of arms or other forms of struggle, is justified, according to the Qur'an, to fight oppression. So, wherever there is oppression, it is encumbent on Muslims to do whatever they can to remove it. *Jihad* is primarily to remove evil and to instil good. How it is done is the problem.

But there are other problems as well. For the Muslim the West belongs to the Dar al-harb, the house of conflict, oppressed by spiritual uncertainty, licensed immorality and wilful materialism, as opposed to Dar al-Islam, those parts of the world where Islam is in the ascendant. For the West, with its folk memory of Ottoman armies at the gates of Vienna, and its tales of the harem, the imposition of Islamic law seems more to do with legalised limb lopping than with a bid for monotheistic religious freedom.

One man's oppression is another man's freedom. Inevitably, Muslim and non-Muslim often talk at cross purposes. Gai Eaton, as a British convert to Islam, has a foot in both camps. He believes that there is a difference of attitude which is more divisive than the difference of religious belief.

For several years he has been lecturing to Christian groups. He started off by thinking that the important differences between the two faiths were doctrinal – the Incarnation, the Trinity, and so on. But he found that these dogmas are relatively unimportant to most Christians today. The real differences are in the climate of belief. Today's Muslim would have felt at home with a Christian in the ages of faith but is very puzzled by the contemporary, sceptical, questioning Christian. The Muslim is more inclined to reserve his questions for the secular world. God is sacrosanct; existing political structures are not.

Western unease about Islam has deep historical roots. Equally, present Islamic anger against the West has been brewing for many years and should not come as a surprise. For the children of this generation, Gai Eaton says, the British Empire is as remote as the Roman Empire. They do not realise that the traumas which Western dominance and hegemony left behind may take centuries to be exhausted or cured. And in a certain sense the whole Third World, which includes much of the Islamic world, is still racked and tormented by the extraordinary impact of Western colonialism. Often you cannot tell to what extent a reaction is specifically Islamic, and to what extent it is typically Third World, an attempt to get one's own back on the former imperialists.

In few areas is the time warp between Islam and the West more immediately evident than in the Islamic attitude towards women. Men may have four wives. Women are only allowed one husband. In heaven the virtuous are attended by amorous doe-eyed houris; handsome young male servants are present but only in the capacity of butlers. On earth the Qur'an accords women the right to be protected rather than to be independent.

But in the seventh century AD the Qur'anic instructions on women were the height of liberality. In the Mecca in which Muhammad grew up women had few rights and no privileges. The practice of killing girl infants was an accepted economic necessity.

The history of Islam accords women positions of honour. The first convert to Islam was Khadija, Muhammad's first wife. One of the first martyrs for Islam was Summaya, an elderly woman who was crushed under a boulder and pierced by spears for her belief in the one God. In heaven Mary, the mother of Jesus, is the leader of the blest.

Muslims claim that the Qur'an alone has set the record straight and freed women from their most ancient and undeserved burden of guilt. Dr Abdel-Haleem points out that in the Old Testament story of the creation of the world, it is Eve who tempts Adam. In the Qur'an it is not Eve who tempts Adam, it is Satan who tempts them both.

Once out of Eden, Islamic women seem to have had a raw deal. Rabiatu Ammah, a Muslim doctoral student from Ghana who studied at the Selly Oak College in Birmingham, when asked whether she felt hard done by as a Muslim woman, replied:

Not at all. I am a Muslim woman who looks at the Qur'an and knows that the Prophet said paradise lies at the feet of women. A man came to the Prophet and asked him, 'Of my parents, which should I give most respect?' And the Prophet said, 'Give it to your mother.' He asked again, 'Who next?' The Prophet said, 'Give it to your mother.' And he asked again, 'Who next?' The Prophet said, 'Give it to your mother.' And he asked again, 'Who next?' And the Prophet said, 'To your father.' So you see how important woman is in Islam. People always misunderstand and misrepresent the status of woman in Islam. We have to distinguish between woman in Islam – in the Qur'an and in the Hadith – and woman in Muslim societies which have been culturally influenced in so many ways. As far as God is concerned, there is no distinction: it is your piety which counts.

There can be little doubt of the Prophet's fondness for women. After Khadija, his first wife, died he married nine or ten times, so in one life Muhammad managed to be the model of monogamy as well as of polygamy. Nowadays many Muslims are defensive about Muhammad's multiple marriages – only Aisha, they point out, was a virgin. The other wives were widows or captives in need of protection. Muhammad himself was less mealy-mouthed. Marriage, he said, was half of religion and when husbands and wives hold hands their sins disappear through their fingers' touch.

But can the romantic chivalry of a seventh-century prophet survive in an age of female education and emancipation? Aisha Johnson, a British convert to Islam living in Pudsey outside Leeds, argues for polygamy from direct personal experience. She is the second Islamic wife of her husband. Polygamy, she believes, is a much under-rated recipe for marital success.

Aisha and her husband are Sunni Muslims. On the whole, the Muslims whom we hear most about on news bulletins are Shi'a or Shi'ite. However monolithic Islam may seem to outsiders, from the earliest days it has suffered division and power struggles. Islam was only united for the lifetime of the Prophet. With his death, ambitious zeal and doubts over who should lead as Caliph split the brotherhood of Muslims into its two main factions.

As Sheikh Jamal, the chief Imam of the Central London Mosque in Regent's Park, explains, immediately after the death of the Prophet, the Muslims were faced with a dilemma. Who was supposed to succeed Muhammad, not as a prophet because that would be decided by God, but as head of the Muslim community. Many Muslims at that time were of the opinion that anyone who was fit and religiously unimpeachable was qualified to be elected. There was also a group, but they were lesser in number, who thought that one of Muhammad's family or a close relative should succeed him, thinking that his goodness might pass on to them.

The majority view prevailed at first, but there were those who thought that the Prophet's cousin Ali would have been a better choice. This division of opinion began as a political question – who was best fitted to succeed, and then acquired a theological dimension, and so the split Islam between the Sunni and the Shi'ite arose.

Professor Seyyed Hossein Nasr, a Shi'ite theologian based in the United States, believes it is important to stress the antiquity of Shi'ism. Both branches of the faith, he says, go back to the origins of Islam, to the life and death of the Prophet. Shi'ism is not a later reaction against Sunnism as say Protestantism was against Catholicism in the sixteenth century. They both began with the question of who was to succeed Muhammad and what the function of that person should be. Should it be someone who would simply carry out the social, civic and military duties of the Prophet and protect the law – which the Sunnis believed, or should it be someone who understood both the inner and outer meaning of the law, and was able to interpret the faith from within, as the Shi'ites believed.

On the basis of these issues a small number of people gradually gathered around the figure of Ali, who was the cousin and son-in-law of the Prophet, in whose father's house the Prophet was brought up and who had been very very close to the Prophet. They thought that Ali should become the Caliph rather than Abu Bakr, the venerable first Caliph of Sunni Islam. From that small beginning the movement grew. Imam Husain, the son of Ali and the grandson of the Prophet, was killed in a battle near the city of Kufa in Baghdad by the army of the Umayyads. The death of the grandson of the Prophet, so beloved by him, caused a great deal of resentment in the Islamic community, Professor Nasr explains, and from then on Shi'ism crystallised as a distinct school within the Islamic world.

When the Shi'ite people of Iran took to the streets and toppled the Peacock Throne, driving the pro-Western Shah of Iran into exile, those startling events brought the strength and fervour of Islam as a radical political force to the centre stage of twentieth-century world politics. But Islam is not the only religion to experience enthusiastic reactionary backlashes. Is it fair to link the ayatollahs of Iran, the Hezbollah of Lebanon and the suicidal terrorists with a general swing towards fundamentalism among believers?

Kenneth Cracknell thinks not. Fundamentalism, he says, is a category that we cannot apply to Islam. All Muslims are fundamentalists in one sense of the word – either you believe the Qur'an is the whole inspired word of God, or you don't; if you don't you are not a Muslim. But there is a group inside Islam who are called Muslim fundamentalists. They are not fundamentalists in the American sense of the word. They are not conservative, rather they want radical political change. They usually become radicalised in Western universities and then return to their own countries. They believe, having suffered Western colonial domination – and most Muslims in the world have been oppressed by the French or the Dutch or the British, and more recently by the economic imperialism of America – that God has given them oil, the petro-dollar, to bring down the West. They feel a sense of urgency because that oil is running out and the West has not yet fallen. To achieve these ends some are prepared to use other methods, one of which is hostage-taking. But such an action is completely un-Qur'anic – Muhammad would certainly not have approved.

Will this urgency take over the rest of Islam? Is there a danger that the Shi'ite enthusiasts will enlist the rest of Islam in a *jihad* against the whole non-Muslim world? Dr Abdel-Haleem thinks that all revolutions are fundamentalist when they start, but that fundamentalism will never prevail in Islam. Historically this has not been the case, and it will not happen now because in the Middle East fundamentalists in the pejorative sense are not in the majority.

Why then has the Shi'a minority captured the news headlines from the Sunni majority? What do the Shi'ites have which the Sunni do not? Professor Nasr explains that Shi'ism

has its own interpretation of Islamic law. It has its own interpretation of theology, of philosophy, and its own collection
of Hadith – or sayings of the Prophet. Shi'ism is based on the
veneration of the Imams who followed the footsteps of the
Prophet, and who represented religious authority after the
death of the Prophet. The 12-Imam Shi'ites comprise the
greatest number of Shi'ites in the world today. They have
twelve Imams of whom the twelfth is now concealed. He is
called the Mahdi, Muhammad al-Mahdi, and will appear
before the end of the world to prepare for the coming of
Christ. Al-Mahdi's coming will be an eschatological event.

But in reality, is it not the case that the notoriety of the
Shi'ites has less to do with Judgement Day and hidden Imams
and more to do with mindless violence and terrorism – the
jihad of the hijack perhaps? Professor Nasr does not think so.
Through most of its history 12-Imam Shi'ism has not been
violent at all. It has been, he says, a gentle, contemplative
branch of Islam and has devoted most of its energy to the sci-
ences of philosophy, theology and the like. What we see
today represents the coming together of the very powerful
historical forces of the present century. The violence we have
seen is not necessarily part of the nature of Shi'ism as 1300
years of history has shown.

There can, however, be no denying the present militant
mood of a large section of Islam – a mood which, according
to Mashuq Ally, is not adequately expressed by the word fundamentalism:

It is regrettable that this word is used so much in the
media because it does not really explain what is happen-
ing within the Muslim world. The word that would be
most appropriate is revival. The movements for Islamic
revival are those which aim to see the rule of God
throughout the world. Every Muslim would like to see

that – otherwise he would not be honest to his commitment to God.

The means towards that depend upon two things: first, the level of faith and secondly the level of consciousness of God. A Muslim's response to situations will depend on the two levels within him or herself. When non-Muslims talk about fundamentalists they are referring to the extremists within the Muslim community, but this is not a true reflection of the Islamic ethos and spirit. Peace, harmony, equilibrium, balance – all these things are encapsulated in this one word *Islam*. If the actions of an individual or a group do not lead to this, it cannot be Islam.

But Islam is not a creed of peace at any price. The Qur'an teaches the duty to fight. Islam is a practical religion for a non-ideal world. As well as the greater *jihad*, the *jihad* of the soul, there is the more mundane lesser *jihad*, the *jihad* of the sword. Muhammad himself was no stranger to the battlefield. He fought in about a hundred battles and always led from the front. He was wounded several times – an arrow pierced his cheek and he lost two teeth at Uhud – though he never killed anyone with his own hand. And the teaching about the lesser *jihad* does not sanction a free for all. There are times to fight and times not to fight, and as Jabal Buaben explains, there is one injustice which overshadows all other as justification for fighting – religious oppression:

> You are created primarily to worship God. If you have been prevented from doing that, then it is your duty to use all available means to uphold the freedom to practise your religion. And that freedom is not a matter just of going to the mosque and coming home, it is a total way of life. So if you find oppression in your social,

family or political life, then you are permitted by the Qur'an to fight against that too.

If the lesser *jihad* can be a tool for social improvement, is there then a Qur'anic sanction for holy war against, for instance, the arguably godless lifestyles of much of the modern world? Professor Nasr says that there is the possibility that the preservation of the Islamic world and the defence of its borders is a *jihad* – but it is only in that sense that the word holy war could be used. It is totally unfair to equate the word *jihad* with holy war and to put it at the heart of Islam, and then to argue that Islam is a religion based on holy war and the sword. The first Crusades were not carried out by Muslims, and non-Islamic civilisations have fought far more wars and killed far more people than Islamic civilisations have done.

Was the recent war between Iran and Iraq a holy war? Iran claimed that it was. Sheikh Jamal says neither side was fighting a *jihad*. Both were in the wrong. We are told by the Prophet, he says, that if two Muslims fight, both the killed and the killer will go to hell.

Recent years have not only witnessed the spectacle of Muslims killing Muslims, but also of Muslims killing non-Muslims in the name of Islam, notably the Baha'i community in Iran. Muslims are always eager to point to the tradition of religious toleration expressed in the Qur'an and seen in history where other faiths survived Muslim rule – in India or the Middle East or North Africa. But there is a Catch 22. Muslims believe that non-Muslims should be free to live in Islamic states provided that they abide by the *Sharia* or law of Islam. Does this mean that although people are not coerced into believing in Islam, they may be required to act as if they do, and may in effect be regarded as second-class citizens? Rabiatu Ammah says not at all. There is nothing to say that the non-Muslim is a second-class citizen under Islamic law.

And she points out that those who have been given a scripture – Jews, Christians and Hindus as well – have to be protected. All minorities have a legal status – they have the right to life and to property. They have to be protected, provided that they submit to the authority of the Muslim government. However, throughout history what has actually happened has not always conformed to the Qur'an or the Hadith.

For many people of many faiths theory and action part company. Sins of omission and commission are not a Muslim prerogative. But Kenneth Cracknell believes that in the West an Islamic *jihad*, in the sense of personal struggle, is inevitable. 'In the West', he says, 'Islam has terrible problems. In Muslim countries it is taken for granted. For instance, nobody says why don't you drink alcohol, it just isn't available. Here, every possibility is open, and Muslim children in British schools know it. What are these young Muslims going to do in this country? They have a choice. The parents don't like it: they would rather set up Muslim schools and Muslim universities, but it is not possible. So they are forced into re-interpretation and new teaching, and they have to learn how to justify Islam and argue from the Qur'an. Insofar as Christians have been able to come to terms with the modern world, they have to help Muslims. On the whole Christians have not done so well, either, so Christians and Muslims are all in the same boat.'

To what extent is that true? The Christian churches are juggling with the problem of women as religious leaders, a problem which seems light years away from the world of Islam where men and women do not even pray together. Will women ever be Imams? Rabiatu Ammah thinks this is unlikely given the deficiencies of men:

I do not think I would want to be an Imam, and a lot of Muslim women I have talked to would not want to be an

Imam because of the very nature of Muslim prayer. We have to bow and we have to prostrate. Muslim women generally feel that they do not want men standing behind them while they are prostrating because sometimes men can be mischievous.

Women Imams are a long way in the future, but Islam will change. It is only in its middle ages and it is spreading, not least in Africa. Professor Nasr says that there are two reasons for this. One is that, to a large extent, Africa still associates Christianity with its colonial past. And although recently the Churches have been trying to divorce themselves from their European identity, nevertheless it will take a long time for that to happen. Secondly, Islam has certain institutions and practices which appeal to what might be called the primordial nature of African religions. Both of these things make it easier for certain parts of Africa to adapt to Islam rather than to Christianity, although from the material point of view, finance and organisation, the Christian churches are much better organised in their missionary activities than the Muslims are.

In recent years, Britain's Muslim community has grown to about 1½ million. This has been caused mainly by immigration rather than by conversion. There are now more Muslims than Methodists in Britain. Islam is now a British faith, but until the outcry over Salman Rushdie's book, *The Satanic Verses*, it kept to itself within the immigrant community.

According to Mashuq Ally, a siege mentality is not necessary. There are distinct advantages to being a Muslim in Britain, he says. It enables Muslims to develop apart from the Muslim community that they have grown up amongst, and to reflect and to re-examine where they stand in their own faith. It provides an opportunity, particularly for young Muslims growing up here, of drawing upon the sources of Islam for

THE PILLARS OF ISLAM

their faith, whereas in their country of origin they would
have drawn on the oral traditions of their families. Also,
because of secularism, they face a challenge – to their way of
life, to their way of thinking and to their spirit. That challenge is important because it enables them to decide where
they stand. Do they stand within Islam or not? Islam is a faith
which wants full commitment, and being in Britain gives the
Muslim an opportunity for examination and reflection. The
drawback perhaps is that there is not the social network to
help people do this, and that is where most Muslims find the
greatest hardship. But for Ally and for many Muslims being
in Britain is a very good opportunity to test their faith.

But opportunities can be double-edged. Sheikh Darsh
thinks that the dangers which are facing all religions, including Christianity and Judaism, are facing Muslims:

> Basically you are free, no-one is interfering in your reli-
> gious observance. I was in Sheffield talking to some
> Muslim students, and some of them were saying, 'Isn't it
> sad that in a non-Muslim country we are free, we can sit
> and talk about Islamic matters without anyone interfer-
> ing in our lives, while in a Muslim country we may not
> be.' Having the luxury of discussing these matters with-
> out looking behind is good. I am fond of saying that if
> we have sound goods we shall be able to market, or at
> least to preserve, our faith. But at the same time the
> social life, the secularism, is eroding the basis of all reli-
> gions whether we like it or not.

Muslims identify secularism as an enemy worth struggling
with as part of the greater *jihad*, and they are surprised at the
lack of action among other religious communities. Mushuq
Ally says that Muslims do feel aggrieved that they do not get
much support from other religious groups who seem to seek a

compromise with secularism rather than face up to it. He thinks that Muslims may be able to offer that leadership whereby people of religion – Christians, Jews, Sikhs, Hindus, no matter to what faith you may belong – may be able to come to terms with secularism and, by so doing, perhaps see a greater level of spirituality within life in Britain which has been missing for many years.

The struggle which is Islam involves faith, prayer, fasting, pilgrimage and also almsgiving – *zakat* – the system of almsgiving whereby the rich give to the poor. Nabilla Kawas believes that this marks out Islam as a creed with answers for a wider community than simply the brotherhood of believers. Islam, she believes, is the only solution for all the present problems of humanity – economic, social and moral.

Lesser *jihads*, the wars of the sword, will come and go. Enthusiasts and extremists driven by ancient prejudices, by ignorance or by genuine injustice will resort to violence. But this should not overshadow the message of the greater *jihad*, the struggle for brotherhood, equity and faith. Islam is not poised for world domination – what need is there when Allah is the Lord of all Creation? But the ideals of Islam reach out beyond its own community. It is a faith in vigorous middle age, still strong in conviction. It has no deference or despair and it is not ashamed of its ambitions.

The human problem is the Islamic problem, says Sheikh Jamal of the Regent's Park Mosque. 'We are part of humanity, we are part of the people. We reflect their pain, we aspire for their hope, and we enjoy their happiness. An undivided, tolerant Islam will be an example to the world.'

My Faith: A Personal Statement

M. S. Modood

My intellectual starting-point is the proposition that the world has a Creator. None of us has willed ourselves into existence; indeed when I came into existence in the belly of my mother, it was weeks before she was even aware of the fact. Our parents may have willed the act of sex, but they had no control over what, if anything, was being created. If we do not choose to be created and have no say over what we will be, it follows that He who wills Creation must lie outside the created world.

Some have held that the Creator is hidden, beyond our grasp, or chooses not to be known. Muslims believe that man is created out of matter, but is infused with the spirit of God, his Creator. We have therefore the potential to receive communications from God and to understand the purpose of Creation. Reason makes us aware that Nature is ordered, not chaotic, that every element, even the tiniest microbe, contributes to a greater ecology and purpose; yet while Reason reveals the presence of purpose, at the same time it makes us aware of the limits of our knowledge. Reason sets in motion a chain of questions and answers, but is of itself unable – at least for ordinary mortals – to come up with any ultimate answers. Faith alone – based on direct communication from Creator to created – can give us the answers and complete the train of reflection set in motion by Reason.

All made things work best when the manufacturer's instructions are followed. To use a car or a lawn-mower in ways that run contrary to the manufacturer's instructions is to abuse it and to risk malfunction and even total breakdown. So it is with Man: our proper functioning depends upon carefully adhering to the dos and don'ts, the step-by-step instructions, of the manufacturer's manual. It is therefore our duty to seek to discover and to obey the Word of the Creator.

Muslims believe that all the prophets are part of a single message, and that when properly understood they will be seen not to be contradicting each other but to be giving emphasis to an aspect of a single universal Truth: God's guidance to Man on how to live on the earth and secure eternity in heaven by means of this life.

Islam is sometimes described by commentators as a young or middle-aged religion. This is far from our own self-understanding. We believe that there is only one religion and that Islam is the clearest statement of God's repeated attempts to communicate the Truth to wayward mankind. We hold Adam to be the first Muslim and we honour all the prophets as prophets of Islam, and respect all the scriptures as divine messages. The Qur'an, however, is the perfect statement and corrects all previous misinterpretations and misunderstandings including, of course, the relationship between Jesus, peace be upon him, and God. Our confidence in the Qur'an is strengthened by the fact that, unlike the Bible, it has been perfectly guarded so there are no different texts in competition with one another, nor new editions which rest on nothing more than linguistic or theological fashions.

A full, learned understanding of the Qur'an is, however,

dependent upon a knowledge of the tradition of which it is the climax. Where the Qur'an is silent, or needs interpretation, or takes something for granted, one must look to the wider tradition in order to understand it. Let me give a simple example: the Qur'an speaks of 'Adam and his wife', yet Muslims have no hesitation in supposing that the unnamed spouse is called Hawa (Eve).

For me, 'the five pillars of Islam' is something of a misnomer. For what is referred to as the first pillar, the profession of faith (*kalma* or *shahada*), is not a pillar but the foundation upon which all else rests. Faith in God as our Creator, in Muhammad, peace be upon him, as the ultimate prophet and model human being, and the Qur'an as the word of God is the foundation of Islam. Unlike the Christian trinity, God, the Qur'an and Muhammad are not joined in one being but form a unity of purpose.

On this foundation rests the four pillars: prayer (*namaz* or *salat*), fasting (*roza* or *sawm*), almsgiving (*zakat*) and pilgrimage (*hajj*). Each of these involves time, effort and some economic cost (including that of lost opportunities). If they did not, they would not be worth doing for they are expressions of love and thus a form of giving, though also, like love, a form of receiving. For on these pillars rests perfect internal harmony and social peace – a harmony and peace that is only possible if one is leading the life for which one was created, like a perfect ball-bearing.

I came to Britain in 1961, full of admiration for the British. In the early days I used to fear that the superiority and attractions of the West would prove too much for a simple-minded people and that we would sell our faith for a share in the obvious advantages of Western civilisation. Thirty years on I no longer have this fear. Early in this century Muhammad 'Abduh, a distinguished religious leader and scholar at Al-Azhar, the centre of Muslim learning in Cairo, after a visit to

Europe wrote: 'In Europe I saw Islam but no Muslims; in Egypt I see many Muslims but no Islam.' Even today the standard of public service, rule of law, democracy, freedom to dissent, and equality in Britain far exceed anything that is found in a Muslim country where dictatorship and brutish coercion, bribery, nepotism and deceit are usual. Yet familiarity with the West increasingly reveals to us – through the many stories in the media about child abuse, rape of the elderly, routine sexual greed and exploitation – the rottenness that lies at the core of this civilisation, contact with which makes us embrace our faith with greater certitude and welcome British converts.

All Muslims long for the creation of truly Muslim societies and polities; but it is our conviction that these will arise from the purity, integrity and strength that flows from submission to God, not from an imitation of the West. It is my sincere belief that this example of faith, modelled on Muhammad, peace be upon him, is the greatest service that Muslims can render Britain and indeed the world. For the wickedness of the human heart will be defeated, not by social reform alone, but by the discipline of faith.

He is the Lord of the Universe, nothing is possible without His knowledge and His will. Islam is complete faith in His sovereignty and justice and complete submission to His will.

Contributors

The authors would like to thank the following individuals who contributed to the Radio Four programme *Pillars of Islam*, broadcast in 1987, who are quoted in this book:

Mashuq Ally, Director of Islamic Studies, St David's University College, Lampeter

Rabiatu Ammah, Muslim scholar, Ghana

Syed Ali Ashraf, Director of The Islamic Academy, Cambridge

Jabal Buaben, Muslim scholar, Ghana

Revd Kenneth Cracknell, formerly secretary of the committee for multi-faith issues at the British Council of Churches

Sheikh Darsh, Muslim scholar and lecturer, London University

Gai Eaton, Muslim convert and Lecturer at the Central London Mosque, Regent's Park

Dr M. A. S. Abdel-Haleem, Lecturer in Arabic, University of London

Sheikh Jamal, Chief Imam of the Central London Mosque, Regent's Park

Aisha Johnson, Muslim convert, Leeds

Nabilla Kawas, Research Fellow at the City University, London

Professor Seyyed Hossein Nasr, George Washington University, Washington DC

Index